The
Palestinian
Lie

Shattering the Myths

O. Isaac

Line Editor: T. Efrati

Contents

Preface

When the horrific massacre of October 7 unfolded, I naively believed the world would unite in solidarity with Israel, which had just endured the most brutal genocide attempt against Jews since the Holocaust. Instead, I watched in disbelief as professors at prestigious universities celebrated the attack, Hollywood stars posted slogans to "free Palestine," and social media erupted with chants and hashtags that justified the slaughter.

What shocked me most wasn't only the cruelty of the attackers, but the speed and ease with which millions of educated, supposedly compassionate Westerners rushed to embrace the Palestinian narrative. It was as if the facts didn't matter. The rape of women, the murder of babies, the sadistic butchering of entire families — all of it was excused with the same line: *"It didn't start on October 7."*

Why? Why did so many people, in the name of justice and human rights, find a way to excuse pure evil?

The Western Liberal Mindset

Over time, I realized something unsettling: in the Western liberal imagination, Palestinians automatically occupy the role of "oppressed natives," and Jews — specifically Zionists — are cast as "white colonizers" who stole their land. This isn't history. It's not even serious analysis. It's a reflex, a ready-made narrative borrowed from Western post-colonial discourse and pasted onto the Middle East without any regard for facts.

For these activists, standing with Palestinians *feels* like standing with the oppressed, the marginalized, the underdog. That feeling is intoxicating because it lets them believe they are righteous crusaders for justice. But their conviction is built not on truth but on lies — lies about demography, lies about migration, lies about who lived where and when.

And because they know little of the region's real history, they fail to recognize the absurdity of the slogans they chant. They repeat *"From the* river to the sea" as if it were a poetic call for freedom, without understanding it is an explicit demand to erase the world's only Jewish state. They repeat *"It didn't start on October 7"* as if it were context, when in reality it is a way to justify barbarism. They say *"Israel was promised to them 3,000 years ago"* — as if Jews were foreigners with a long-expired claim — thereby erasing thousands of years of continuous Jewish presence in their ancestral homeland.

The Echo Chamber of Social Media

This blindness is amplified in the echo chamber of social media. Algorithms reward outrage, not truth. A clever slogan is shared, repeated, and echoed until its "truthiness" overwhelms actual truth. The more people repeat the lie, the more convinced they become of its reality.

On TikTok, Instagram, and Twitter, the cycle is predictable: one influencer coins a phrase, it goes viral, and millions repeat it without once stopping to ask what it means. I have debated countless people online who seemed intelligent, articulate, and even well-read — until you asked them to define the slogans they were shouting. That was when the conversation collapsed.

Historical facts are dismissed out of hand as "hasbara." Archival records, census data, and eyewitness accounts become meaningless because they don't align with the narrative. When you present documents showing Arab immigration during the British Mandate outpaced Jewish immigration, the answer is: *"Hasbara."* When you cite Ottoman censuses showing Jews were a majority in Jerusalem long before Zionism, the answer is: *"Hasbara."* And if you persist in defending Israel online, the assumption comes quickly: you must be getting paid by Israel, or by AIPAC, or by some shadowy "Zionist lobby." This is not healthy skepticism. It is antisemitism reborn — the idea that Jews cannot speak truth without being accused of conspiracy and corruption.

Breaking Down the Slogans

Take *"From the river to the sea."* On campuses and in protests, it is chanted with joy, painted on banners, worn proudly on T-shirts. When confronted, many of its chanters claim it is just a vague call for "freedom." But freedom for whom? Certainly not for Jews. The Jordan River to the Mediterranean Sea encompasses all of Israel. There is no room in that vision for the Jewish state. The slogan is not about coexistence — it is a call for elimination. Yet Western liberals, who pride themselves on inclusivity and tolerance, chant it with no awareness of its genocidal implications.

Then there is *"It didn't start on October 7."* This phrase has become a shield for denial. It is meant to redirect attention away from Hamas's atrocities and onto a long list of grievances, real or imagined, against Israel. But in practice it functions as justification: *because something happened before, the rape of women and the slaughter of families is excusable.* It transforms murderers into "resistance fighters" and turns the victims into the guilty.

And then there is the favorite trope: *"Israel was promised to the Jews 3,000 years ago."* Spoken with a mocking tone, as if Jews were ridiculous for claiming an ancient connection. But that phrasing itself is a distortion, suggesting that Jews disappeared for 3,000 years and only recently reappeared. The truth — that Jews lived continuously in the land, prayed daily for Jerusalem, returned in waves across centuries, and never relinquished their identity — is erased with a smug slogan.

The Hypocrisy of Selective Outrage

What makes this all the more infuriating is the hypocrisy. Western activists scream endlessly about Palestinians, but remain silent about Kurds denied a homeland, Yazidis slaughtered by ISIS, or Uyghurs imprisoned in Chinese camps. None of these tragedies trend on TikTok with catchy hashtags. None inspire students to shut down universities. Only the Jewish state provokes such obsessive rage.

The reason is clear: in the Western progressive imagination, Jews are not allowed to be victims. Jews with power, Jews defending themselves, Jews surviving against the odds — this makes people uncomfortable. So instead of celebrating Jewish survival, they recast it as oppression.

The Rationalization of October 7

Then came October 7. Hamas's atrocities should have ended the debate. For anyone truly committed to human rights, the images of slaughtered families, mutilated women, and kidnapped babies should have been undeniable proof of evil.

But instead of confronting this evil, many of those who had always imagined themselves as standing with "the oppressed" scrambled to protect their self-image. Because if Hamas were evil — and if they had supported Hamas — then they themselves would be complicit in evil. That was intolerable. So they twisted reality. They said: *"It didn't start on October 7."* They said: *"This was resistance."*

They refused to watch the videos of the massacre. They tore down posters of kidnapped Israeli women and children. They accused the victims of genocide and called the Jews *Nazis*. In one grotesque inversion, the people who had just endured an attempt at genocide were branded as the perpetrators of genocide.

This was not just ignorance. It was willful blindness, a psychological defense mechanism. To preserve their self-image as "good people fighting for the oppressed," they had to deny the obvious evil committed in broad daylight. They had to rewrite reality in real time.

Why I Wrote This Book

It was in the middle of this madness that I decided to write this book. Because the lies are not new. They have existed for decades, carefully cultivated and repeated until they hardened into dogma. What has changed is how quickly and broadly they spread. With social media, lies can reach millions within hours, unchallenged, repeated by people who never once bothered to ask if the slogans they chanted actually made sense.

This book is my response. It is not just a collection of counter-arguments, but a demolition of the myths that have dominated the discourse. It is a record of history, demography, and lived reality — facts that cannot be wished away by hashtags.

If you are reading this, it is probably because you are willing to question. You may already suspect that the story you've been told is not the whole truth. My goal is not only to present the evidence, but to expose the mechanisms by which lies become "truth" in the modern imagination.

A Final Word

Let me be clear: defending Israel is not propaganda. It is defending truth against a tide of distortion. It is rejecting the oldest hatred in its newest disguise.

This book is my contribution to fighting that lie. If even one reader walks away seeing the myths for what they are — manipulations, not history — then it will have been worth writing.

Introduction

Ladies and gentlemen of the jury, let us begin with the central claim that dominates today's conversation about Israel and Palestine: *"Jews were foreign colonizers who invaded a native Arab land and stole it."*

This claim is repeated so often —on protest signs, in United Nations speeches, and across social media feeds — that it is treated as settled truth. Western liberals automatically assume Palestinians are the oppressed and Zionists the oppressors. They imagine an ancient, stable Muslim population that lived in Palestine "since time immemorial," suddenly uprooted by waves of Jewish immigrants who arrived with Western backing to dispossess them — while mocking Jews as outsiders clinging to a promise "from 3,000 years ago," conveniently ignoring that Jews never left.

But what if this entire story was a **lie**?

For millennia, Jewish life in the Land of Israel was unbroken — from Hebron to Tiberias, from Safed to Jerusalem, where Jews often formed the majority long before modern Zionism began.

What if I told you that, on the eve of the First Aliyah (the first Zionist immigration wave of pioneers, beginning in 1881), **Jews actually outnumbered native Muslims** in the territory that would become Israel?

What if I told you that the Arab population inside pre-1967 Israel was, for the most part, the result of **late Ottoman and British-era migration**, not ancient indigeneity?

And what if I told you that, after Zionism began, **Arab immigration into Palestine exceeded Jewish immigration from Europe**? That the supposed "native" population actually swelled because of the jobs, infrastructure, and prosperity that Jews created?

The Myth of an Ancient Native Majority

The Palestinian narrative rests on the idea that Arabs were there first, that Jews arrived later, and that Zionism displaced a settled population. It is a powerful myth because it appeals to Western minds shaped by colonial guilt: brown "natives" against white "colonizers."

But the actual records — census data, Ottoman land codes, traveler accounts, British commissions — tell a very different story.

We will show that in the mid-1800s, before Zionism even began, Jews were already the dominant population in key cities like Jerusalem, Safed, and Tiberias. In Jerusalem, the 1922 British census — taken just after the end of Ottoman rule — showed a nearly **3-to-1 Jewish majority.** And this was no anomaly: every reliable count since the first Ottoman survey in 1844 confirmed Jews as the majority in Jerusalem.

Far from being "colonial newcomers," Jews were the demographic backbone of the land's most important city for at least a century before Israel's birth.

We will also show that the supposed Arab "native" population was far smaller than today's myths suggest. In reality, much of the Muslim population in the land that became Israel descended from **late Ottoman migration waves , which occurred largely in parallel with Zionist immigration from Europe**: Egyptians brought in under Muhammad Ali of Egypt, Bedouin tribes resettled by the Ottomans, Maghrebis from North Africa, Circassians and Bosnians expelled from the Balkans, Hauranis from southern Syria, Turks from Anatolia, Metawali Shi'a from Lebanon, and Levantine Arabs who arrived for work opportunities. Once these groups are accounted for, the number of genuinely native Muslim families shrinks dramatically.

So dramatically, in fact, that **Jews outnumbered them on the eve of the First Aliyah in 1881.**

The claim that Zionists invaded a full land collapses when you look at the numbers. Palestine was not overflowing with rooted Arab families. It was, in Zionist words, **"a land of no people for a people without a land."**

The Land Was Empty — and the Records Prove It

Mark Twain, traveling through the land in 1867, described desolation: "A desolate country whose soil is rich enough, but is given over wholly to weeds... A silent mournful expanse... We never saw a human being on the whole route."

He was not alone. Dozens of travelers, consuls, and geographers reported the same: barren hills, malaria-infested swamps, and tiny clusters of people scratching out a living. The land was underpopulated, underdeveloped, and neglected. And this was no isolated impression — later in this book we will present account after account from European, American, and even Ottoman observers, all confirming that Palestine before Zionism was a sparsely populated and desolate land.

We will dive into the Ottoman land codes of 1858, which classified most of Palestine as *miri* — state-owned land under the Sultan in Istanbul — or *mawat* land, literally "dead land," uncultivated and uninhabited. These categories matter because they prove ownership claims were paper-thin. If Arabs truly had deep ancestral ties, why were their lands legally classified as belonging to the Sultan or as wasteland?

And let us be clear: the land Zionists bought was purchased **legally**. Every acre was acquired — often at exorbitant prices —through the proper legal channels under Ottoman law. In fact, many purchases involved *mawat* land — "dead land" that was uncultivated, uninhabited, and classified as wasteland by the Ottomans, which could be redeemed and developed through legal purchase. There is not a shred of evidence of a single home or farm stolen illegally. The myth of theft evaporates under Ottoman law itself.

The truth is simple: **Zionists did not dispossess natives. They revived a desolate land.**

Arab Immigration Outpaced Jewish Immigration

Another myth claims: *"Jews flooded in from Europe and overwhelmed the Arabs."* The reality? The opposite.

During the British Mandate (1920–1948), official records show that **Arab immigration into Palestine was larger than Jewish immigration.** Arabs from Syria, Lebanon, Egypt, and Transjordan poured in, drawn by the prosperity Zionist settlers created. While Jewish immigrants were carefully documented, Arabs often crossed borders on foot, unregistered.

Critics condemned European Jews for "flooding" into British Palestine while fleeing pogroms and the Holocaust. But those same critics ignored the **tens of thousands of Egyptians brought in by Muhammad Ali**, and the **tens of thousands of Bedouin tribes forcibly relocated by the Ottomans** in the 19th century — numbers that dwarf early Jewish immigration.

Even Arab leaders have admitted this truth. **Fathi Hammad**, a former Hamas Interior Minister, openly declared on Al-Hayat TV that *"half of Palestinians are Egyptians and the other half are Saudis."* When your own officials concede your identity is a recent patchwork of migrations, how can the world continue to pretend otherwise?

In Jaffa, Haifa, and the Galilee, Arab populations surged not because they were "returning home," but because Jews had turned malaria-ridden swamps into farmland, built electric plants, ports, and railways, and created jobs.

We will demonstrate this with numbers: censuses, labor reports, and migration records. The data will speak for itself.

The Myth of British Support

You have heard another myth: *"The British created Israel."* This myth collapses almost instantly once you look at the evidence.

Yes, Britain issued the **Balfour Declaration in 1917**, expressing support for "the establishment in Palestine of a national home for the Jewish people." But almost as soon as the ink dried, that promise began to unravel. Successive British governments — beginning with Churchill's partition of the Mandate and continuing through a series of restrictive policies — systematically walked back the commitment.

Did you know that in 1939, as Hitler prepared his Final Solution, the British issued a White Paper that **blocked Jewish immigration** to Palestine — capping it at 75,000 over five years, an average of just 15,000 per year — while millions of Jews were being slaughtered in Europe?

Did you know that Britain **executed Jewish resistance fighters** — young men who fought for the right of Holocaust survivors to enter their homeland?

Did you know that Britain **armed and trained the Arab Legion**, the very army that invaded Israel in 1948 under the command of a British general, **John Glubb**? And not just Glubb — dozens of British officers led its units. They were not mercenaries freelancing for Arab kings, but active-duty officers, appointed by Britain, paid by Britain, and ultimately reporting to the British Crown.

Did you know that when Israel declared independence in May 1948, the United States, Britain, and all Western powers **imposed an arms embargo** — while Arab armies were flooded with weapons from British and French stockpiles?

How can Israel be called a Western "colonial project" when the entire Western world refused to sell it arms, while openly supporting its enemies?

The Case We Will Make

This book is not just a rebuttal. It is a demolition.

We will present evidence — census records, migration data, consular reports, traveler diaries, Ottoman legal codes — showing that:

✓ Jews outnumbered native Muslims before Zionism.
✓ The land that became Israel was sparsely populated, undeveloped.
✓ Arab immigration during Zionism outpaced Jewish immigration.
✓ Britain did not create Israel; Britain betrayed the Jews at every turn.
✓ Far from being a colonial outpost, Israel was born in defiance of Western obstruction.

And we will tackle myth after myth:

o That Palestine was "always Arab."
o That Palestinians are the indigenous population.
o That Zionists "stole land."
o That Israel is a Western colonial project.

By the time we are finished, the verdict will be clear: the story told on campuses and on social media is not history. It is propaganda.

A Final Word Before the Evidence

The trial begins here. In the chapters that follow, we will cross-examine the claims one by one. We will put the slogans on the witness stand and force them to face the evidence.

This is not just about history. It is about the present. Because as long as these lies dominate, Jews defending their homeland will continue to be slandered as colonizers, and terrorists will continue to be excused as "resistance fighters."

This book exists to end that lie.

A Quick Note on Terminology

Before we begin, let's clarify an important point: There was never an independent Arab country in this region called Palestine. Since the Romans renamed Judea to Palestine nearly 1,900 years ago, it has been a province under various empires. From the Roman Empire to the Ottoman Empire, the area has always been under the control of external powers.

The British revived the name "Palestine" in 1920 when they took control of the region. Before this, the name had been out of official use for nearly two millennia. The Romans originally renamed "Judea" to "Syria Palaestina" in 135 CE following a Jewish revolt, aiming to erase the land's Jewish identity. The British chose the name "Palestine" for its familiarity to Europeans through ancient Roman maps and literature.

Throughout this book, when referring to the pre-1948 period, I'll use terms like Jews, Arabs, and Muslims to describe the population groups. During the British Mandate, the term "Palestinian" applied broadly to anyone living within the British Mandate for Palestine, regardless of religion or ethnicity. For simplicity, we will use the term "Palestine" to describe the land that became the British Mandate for Palestine in 1920.

Buckle Up

This book is for those who want to know the truth, even if it's uncomfortable. I promise it will be worth your time. Prepare to have your understanding of this conflict turned upside down, and to see the evidence that has been buried beneath decades of propaganda, myths, and outright lies.

Chapter 1

The Ottoman Occupation (1516-1917)

The Ottoman Empire, one of history's great superpowers, spanned three continents and ruled over more than thirty modern nations. Within the empire, there were no national borders or sovereign states as we know them today. The empire was divided into administrative regions called *sanjaks*, which were part of larger provinces (*vilayets*).

For 400 years, from 1516 to 1917, the region later referred to as the British Mandate for Palestine was under Islamic Ottoman rule. Yet, during this time, there was no political or administrative entity officially called "Palestine." Instead, key regions of what was later called Palestine were included in the **Sanjak of Jerusalem**, which was part of the larger Vilayet of Damascus or the Vilayet of Beirut, depending on the period.

Let me set the stage here: the term "Palestine" was mostly a Western construct, used by European travelers or cartographers, and it didn't represent any specific political or geographic reality under Ottoman administration. This is important because many of the modern claims about Palestine hinge on this supposed distinct identity that, frankly, didn't exist between the Jewish Bar Kokhba Revolt (135 CE) and 1920.

Palestine was never home to one continuous, ancient population. It was a crossroads of empires—a place continually repopulated by new rulers, migrants, and conquerors. Throughout its history, the land's inhabitants changed with every major conquest. Peoples came and went; villages disappeared and reappeared; frontiers shifted; and new populations replaced old ones.

One of the clearest examples of this transformation occurred during the **Crusader period** (1099–1291). When the European Crusaders captured Jerusalem in 1099, they founded the **Kingdom of Jerusalem**, a Christian monarchy that lasted nearly two centuries. The

1

victory was followed by widespread massacres of the city's Muslim and Jewish residents—tens of thousands were slaughtered or expelled, and Jerusalem was repopulated with European settlers from France, Italy, and Germany. The Crusaders established new towns, churches, and fortresses, introducing a Latin Christian culture utterly foreign to the region's previous population.

When the Muslim leader **Saladin** recaptured Jerusalem in 1187, he reversed the Crusader expulsions and brought in new settlers from Egypt, Syria, and Mesopotamia. Later, under the **Mamluks** (13th–16th centuries), much of the land had become depopulated again due to war, plague, and neglect. The Mamluks repopulated key cities by relocating tribes, soldiers, and families from across the Islamic world.

This pattern of conquest, depopulation, and resettlement repeated itself for centuries—under the Romans, Byzantines, Crusaders, Ayyubids, Mamluks, and finally the Ottomans. Each wave reshaped the human landscape of the region, leaving behind ruins, abandoned villages, and new populations with no ancient roots in the soil they now occupied.

By the time the Ottomans arrived in 1516, large parts of the country were already sparsely inhabited and underdeveloped. Ottoman officials themselves described wide areas of the land as barren, overgrown, and nearly empty of permanent settlement.

This is the historical backdrop against which the modern story begins. When the first Zionist pioneers arrived in the late 19th century, they did not find a thriving, timeless Arab society. They encountered a neglected frontier that had been repeatedly emptied and refilled for centuries—a land still recovering from centuries of decline under imperial rule.

The Beginning of Zionism

Our story begins in 1881, 67 years before Israel was created, the year of the First Aliya — the first Zionist immigration wave of pioneers. At the time, Palestine was under Ottoman rule.

Before diving into the details, let's confront a pervasive myth — that Zionism was a colonial project and that Jews "stole" Arab land. Nothing could be further from the truth. Zionism was not about colonization; it was a movement of return — a people reclaiming its ancestral homeland, the very land central to Jewish identity for millennia.

When the Zionist movement began, early pioneers often described Palestine as *"a land without a people for a people without a land."* Critics today like to dismiss that phrase as propaganda, but let us put it on trial. Was the land really empty? Was it home to an ancient, rooted Arab nation, as modern slogans claim? Or was it sparsely populated, underdeveloped, and largely barren, exactly as the pioneers described? In the pages ahead, we will examine overwhelming historical evidence that proves the **Zionists were right**.

Let's present the evidence — three exhibits that, together, expose the myth once and for all.

Exhibit A:
The legal state of the land itself under Ottoman law.

Exhibit B:
Eyewitness accounts from travelers, consuls, and geographers.

Exhibit C:
Census records and documented immigration waves that reveal when and how the population truly grew.

Before we examine the evidence, let's pause on what this claim really means. If the land was truly sparsely populated and neglected, then the entire modern narrative of a thriving "native Palestinian nation" crumbles before it even begins. The Ottoman records, the testimony of foreign travelers, and the censuses themselves are not Zionist propaganda — they are neutral, historical facts. And facts have no ideology. With that in mind, let us turn to our first line of evidence: the legal state of the land under Ottoman law.

Exhibit A ("A Land with No People")
The State of the Land: 80% Classified as *Dead Land* ("*Mawat*")

Critics love to mock the phrase "a land without a people," claiming it was Zionist propaganda. But what did the early pioneers actually find — a thriving Arab nation or a sparsely inhabited, neglected land of swamps and deserts? The Ottomans themselves gave us the answer, and their records leave no room for doubt.

I will focus here on the territory that became Israel within its **pre-1967 borders**. This does not include the West Bank and Gaza, which came under Israeli control only after the Six-Day War of 1967. Between 1948 and 1967, the West Bank was under Jordanian rule (formally annexed in 1950) and Gaza under Egyptian occupation. Our focus is the land that made up the heart of the State of Israel from its birth in 1948 until the watershed year of 1967.

Ottoman Land Classifications

To understand how populated or empty this land was, we must begin with the Ottoman legal framework. The **Ottoman Land Code of 1858** divided territory into several categories. Four of these are critical to our discussion:

- **Mawat ("dead land"):** uncultivated, uninhabited, lying beyond village boundaries, legally wasteland until redeemed by purchase and development.

- **Miri:** state land, owned by the Sultan, which individuals could cultivate and pass on to heirs but never own outright.

- **Mulk:** true private freehold property — rare, mostly in cities or small orchards.

- **Waqf:** land dedicated as religious endowment for mosques or institutions.

Modern debates often skip over these distinctions, but they are decisive. If most of the country was legally classified as *mawat* or *miri*, then it was not ancestral farmland rooted in generations of Arab peasants. It was either barren wasteland or property of the Sultan.

Mawat Land — Dead Land on a Massive Scale

The largest category by far was *mawat*. By definition, *mawat* meant land beyond villages, uncultivated and uninhabited. A farmer could not claim it; only by purchasing and developing it could it be redeemed.

In the territory of Israel's pre-1967 borders, this classification covered the overwhelming majority of the land. Regional surveys confirm that **at least 80% of the country was officially *mawat* under Ottoman law**. Consider the following:

The **Negev Desert**, about 12,000 square kilometers, makes up nearly 60% of Israel's area. Under Ottoman law it was entirely *mawat* — empty desert scrub, without villages, farms, or permanent settlement. Add to this the **Arava Valley**, another 1,700 km² stretching to Eilat, also wholly barren, and we are already past two-thirds of the country classified as dead land.

Further north lay the swampy **Hula Valley** (150 km²) and the **Jezreel Valley** (380 km²), both notorious for malaria and unusable soils. Ottoman records treated these as *mawat* until Zionist pioneers drained and reclaimed them. The **Jordan Valley** (2,000 km²) and **Beit She'an Valley** (250 km²) were largely saline or swampy, used for grazing at best, and fell mostly under *mawat*.

The coastal regions were no different. The **Sharon Plain** (1,800 km²) was dominated by malaria swamps and belts of shifting sand dunes. South of it stretched the **Ashdod–Ashkelon sand belt**, about 400 km², completely barren until stabilized by afforestation in the 20th century.

Even in the supposedly "fertile" Galilee, vast tracts were wasteland. The **Lower Galilee** (4,000 km²) consisted of rocky hillsides and barren slopes, half of it uncultivated. The rugged **Upper and Western Galilee** (1,000 km²) was even more hostile terrain, with perhaps 40% officially *mawat*. Moving westward, the **Shfela foothills** (2,000 km²) and **Lachish region** (500 km²) were partially cultivated but still contained large stretches of uncultivated scrub — 40–50% *mawat*. Finally, the **Besor region** (1,000 km²) in the northern Negev remained semi-desert scrub, about 70% *mawat*.

When all these regions are added together, the result is unambiguous: **over 80% of the territory of Israel within the 1967 borders was officially classified as mawat by Ottoman law.**

When all these regions are added together, the cumulative picture is overwhelming. The Negev alone accounts for about 12,000 km² (≈58% of Israel). Add the Arava, the Jordan Valley, the Lower and Upper Galilee, the Sharon Plain, the Ashdod–Ashkelon coastal dunes, the Shfela, the Lachish region, the Besor, plus the swampy Hula, Jezreel, and Beit She'an valleys. Taken as a whole, these areas cover well over 16,700 km² out of Israel's total 20,770 km² within the 1967 borders.

That works out to roughly **80% of the land officially classified by the Ottomans as *mawat* — dead, uncultivated, uninhabited land.**

Miri Land — The Sultan's Property

The next significant category was *miri*. This land, making up **15–18% of Israel's pre-1967 territory**, was not private property but state land belonging to the Ottoman Sultan. Farmers and villagers could cultivate it, but they did not own it in the Western sense. They were tenants of the state. When Zionists purchased such land, they typically bought cultivation rights from absentee landlords in Beirut or Damascus — not from age-old village families with freehold deeds.

Mulk Land — Rare and Urban

True private freehold (*mulk*) was exceedingly rare. It represented no more than **2–5% of the land in Palestine as a whole**, concentrated mostly in urban plots around Jerusalem, Jaffa, Haifa, Tiberias, and a handful of small orchards. There were no sweeping estates of mulk farmland in the countryside.

What the Land Classifications Prove

Most modern activists shouting about 'stolen land' have never opened the Ottoman Land Code, and wouldn't know the difference between *miri* and *mawat*. They repeat slogans, not facts. We will dismantle the ownership myth later. For now, the only point that matters is this: according to the Ottomans' own records, the land was overwhelmingly barren and sparsely populated.

The very fact that over **80% of the country was legally defined as *mawat*** — dead, uncultivated, uninhabited land — is itself proof of sparseness. By Ottoman law, land could only be recorded as *mawat* if it lay beyond village boundaries and lacked cultivation or permanent settlement. That such a vast share of the territory fell into this category demonstrates that Palestine was not densely settled. It was not the homeland of a large, stable Arab nation. It was a neglected frontier of deserts, swamps, rocky hills, and dunes.

The classification speaks louder than any slogan: if 80% of the land was officially wasteland, then the people were few and scattered. Long before Zionism, the Ottomans' own records testify that this was a thinly populated, underdeveloped land — exactly as the early pioneers described it.

Exhibit B ("A Land with No People")
Accounts from Travelers: A Desolate Land

If the Ottoman records prove that most of Palestine was legally classified as wasteland, eyewitness testimony confirms it in vivid detail. For more than a century, travelers, diplomats, and geographers from across the Western world described the same conditions: a land thinly inhabited, neglected, and desolate. Let us hear their testimony.

Richard Pococke (1738):

> "A land forsaken and desolate, where villages are few and far between, and vast tracts lie empty of people."

Thomas Shaw (1730s):

> "In a state of decay, its fields empty and villages abandoned, a country that seems to have lost its people."

Constantin-François Volney (1783–1785):

> "The Holy Land is a ruined and desolate place... We find nothing but remnants of past greatness, a land reduced to barrenness and solitude."

Carsten Niebuhr (1766–1767):

"Thinly inhabited and ill-cultivated... the few villages are miserable and poor."

John Lloyd Stephens (1836–1837):

"A silent and mournful land, with little sign of human habitation."

Alphonse de Lamartine (1832):

"...outside of the gates of Jerusalem we saw nothing living. We heard no living sound. We found the same emptiness, the same silence as if nature itself had withdrawn from the borders of the Holy City... This land is now a solitude."

Alexander Keith (1843):

"Waste and desolate... a land which for centuries has mourned without inhabitants."

Edward Robinson (1838):

"Long stretches of the country are destitute of inhabitants."

Victor Guérin (1850s–1870s):

"Many areas of Palestine are almost deserted, with only a handful of miserable villages scattered across great distances."

M.W. Thomson (1859):

"It is a fact that we may not ignore, that Palestine is now almost a desert.... The country is in great measure empty of inhabitants...

There are no trees, no verdure, no flowers, no streams, and, therefore, no inhabitants."

Mark Twain (1867):

"There is not a solitary village throughout its whole extent—not for thirty miles in either direction. There are two or three small clusters of Bedouin tents, but not a single permanent habitation. One may ride ten miles, hereabouts, and not see ten human beings.... A desolation is here that not even imagination can grace with the pomp of life and action... We never saw a human being on the whole route."

On Bethlehem, Twain added:

"There is no hum of life. There is no human activity of any kind."

Karl Beeker (1876):

"An empty country in need of cultivation and population."

Laurence Oliphant (1887):

"The country is to a considerable degree empty of inhabitants and therefore its greatest need is that of a body of population."

He continued:

"A region more desolated than this could scarcely be conceived."

Other Testimonies Across the Centuries

The list of witnesses goes on. The French historian **Victor Guérin** wrote of deserted plains. The British consul **James Finn** in the 1850s lamented that the countryside was "in ruin, its villages miserable." The German geographer **Karl Ritter** described Palestine as "largely void of people." Explorers like **Alexander Keith**, **Edward Robinson**, **John Lloyd Stephens**, and **M.W. Thomson** all echoed the same theme.

From the 1700s through the late 1800s, observers as diverse as **Carsten Niebuhr (1760s)**, **Volney (1780s)**, **Pococke (1730s)**, **Thomas Shaw (1730s)**, and later **Oliphant (1880s)** painted a consistent picture: Palestine was thinly populated, often empty, and desolate.

Arab Population in the West Bank under Ottoman Rule

Even in the West Bank — which later became the core of Palestinian Arab settlement — the Ottoman tax records prove just how thin the population was.

- In the **district of Hebron**, today home to more than **700,000 people**, the Ottoman count was just **3,000–5,000**.

- In the **district of Nablus**, now with over **440,000 residents**, records show only **9,000–10,000 people** lived there.

These were not cities. They were small clusters of villages in rugged hills, often isolated from one another, struggling against disease and banditry.

A Land Struggling to Sustain Life

Life was precarious. Malaria-infested swamps killed off entire settlements. Roads were in ruins, and there was almost no healthcare outside Jerusalem. Infant mortality was catastrophic, and sanitation was abysmal. Even the few existing villages were fragile, subject to depopulation when harvests failed or epidemics struck.

The Verdict of the Travelers

If the Ottomans' records show the land was wasteland, the travelers' voices show what that looked like on the ground: valleys without villages, plains without farms, swamps that choked life, deserts stretching for miles without a soul in sight. Again and again, explorers, consuls, geographers, and poets reported the same thing — Palestine was sparsely populated, desolate, and in decline.

These men were not Zionists. They came from Europe and America, decades before the Zionist movement began, with no agenda but to record what they saw. And what they saw was not a thriving Arab homeland, but a country abandoned by history, its villages scattered and its fields empty.

From Pococke in the 1730s to Oliphant in the 1880s, their testimony is unanimous: Palestine was not the heartland of a great nation, but a land waiting to be revived. The verdict is clear. The land was barren, the population thin, the country desolate.

Exhibit C ("A Land with No People")
Census Records and Documented Immigration Waves

Let's tackle the claim that the Arab population of Palestine was ancient and native. The truth is that much of it arrived only in the late Ottoman period, through government resettlement programs and simple economic migration.

To prove this, we'll trace the major Muslim migration waves that came into the land during the 1800s, focusing on the area that later became Israel within the 1967 borders. The analysis is based on the work of respected Ottoman historians — **Justin McCarthy, Kemal Karpat, and Alexander Schölch** — whose research used Ottoman census data, tax records, and other official archives.

This section is drawn from my detailed study, *Rethinking Nativeness in Late Ottoman Palestine*, available at *www.ThePalestinianLieBook.com* for anyone who wants the full technical version.

What Do We Mean by "Native"?

In this book, *native* means the settled families whose roots in the land go back **before 1830**. That cutoff matters. It excludes the Bedouin tribes that came from the Arabian Peninsula and all the later groups — Egyptians, Algerians, Hauranis, Circassians, Turks, Balkan refugees, Metawali, Maghrebis, and others — whose arrival after 1830 dramatically changed the population map.

The Core Idea

By using the 1922 British Mandate census as our baseline and tracing back the known migration waves under Ottoman rule, we find that **most Muslims then living in the land were descendants of recent arrivals**. Once those later groups are accounted for, the number of long-rooted Muslim families becomes surprisingly small — in fact, smaller than the old Jewish communities ("Old Yishuv") already living there at the same time.

When we adjust the 1922 numbers to remove these migrant groups and then project backward to 1881 (the eve of the First Zionist immigration wave), we find that **the native Muslim population was likely smaller than the established Jewish community** — showing that Jews were not newcomers but one of the oldest and most continuous populations in the land.

How We'll Do It

1. Find how many Muslims lived within Israel's 1967 borders in 1922 ($\approx$ 277,000).

2. Reconstruct the main 19th-century migration waves, estimate when they arrived, and project their numbers forward using a 1 percent annual growth rate.

3. Subtract those migrant-origin populations from the 1922 total to see how many truly "native" Muslims remained.

4. Roll that number back to 1881 to see what it looked like before Zionist immigration began.

5. Compare it with the native Jewish population (*Old Yishuv*) on the eve of the first Zionist immigration wave ($\approx$ 25,000–27,000).

Step 1: How Many Muslims Lived Inside Israel's 1967 Borders in 1922?

The starting point for our analysis is the **1922 British Mandate census** — the first modern headcount of the land. It recorded **590,890 Muslims** across all of Palestine. But remember: that included areas like the **West Bank and Gaza**, which were not part of Israel's 1967 borders. To get a fair baseline, we have to carefully strip those out.

The process is straightforward:

1. We remove the sub-districts that lay entirely outside Israel's later borders, such as Hebron, Ramallah, Bethlehem, Nablus, and Jenin. That subtraction alone accounts for **205,489 Muslims** who were never inside Israel's borders.

2. We then handle the "borderline" districts that straddled the frontier — **Jerusalem, Tulkarm, and Gaza** — by going village by village and separating the communities that fell inside Israel from those that fell outside.

Here's what the data shows:

- In the **Jerusalem district**, only five villages on the western side of the city fell inside Israel: Lifta, Deir Yassin, Malha, Ein Karem, and Qalunya. Together they had just ≈**4,500 Muslims**. The rest — about **36,000** — lived outside.

- In the **Tulkarm district**, most Muslims lived east of the border, but a cluster of villages like Tayibe, Tira, Qalansuwa, and Kafr Saba fell inside. Their combined total comes to about **6,000–8,000**.

- In the **Gaza district**, only the northern belt of villages was inside Israel — including al-Majdal (Ashkelon), Isdud (Ashdod), Bayt Daras, Hamama, Barbara, Hiribya, Jiyya, Julis, and others. Together they accounted for **17,752 Muslims**. The bulk of Gaza's population — more than **52,000** — was outside.

When you put it all together, the result is clear:

- Outside Israel's pre-1967 borders (West Bank + Gaza + East Jerusalem, etc.): ≈**314,000 Muslims**

- Inside Israel's pre-1967 borders ≈**277,000 Muslims**

This figure of **277,000 Muslims** is our baseline for 1922.

Cross-Check: Independent Confirmation from Fred Gottheil

Skeptics may ask: *"But how do we know these numbers aren't just one person's reconstruction?"* That's a fair question. Fortunately, we have an independent check.

In the early 1970s, economist **Fred M. Gottheil** at the University of Illinois published a detailed analysis of the 1922 census, adjusting it to match the borders of pre-State Israel. He did this by reassigning populations at the village level — carefully separating out communities inside and outside the later frontier — and, importantly, excluding the nomadic Bedouin of Beersheba, since they did not represent settled, permanent inhabitants.

Gottheil's calculation produced a total of **321,866 Arabs** living inside what became Israel. But what proportion of these Arabs were Muslims, as opposed to Christians?

Using the census tables for the districts fully inside Israel (Beersheba, Jaffa, Ramleh, Beisan, Acre, Haifa, Safad, Tiberias, and Nazareth), we find about **286,000 Muslims** and **56,000 Christians**. That's a Muslim share of roughly **84%**.

Now apply that percentage to Gottheil's 321,866 Arabs, and the result is clear: about **270,000 Muslims** within Israel's 1967 borders in 1922.

The Verdict

This figure sits right on top of our own reconstruction (≈277,000). Two completely different methods — one going district by district, the other retrofitting the census to Israel's borders — both land in the same range.

The convergence leaves little doubt: by 1922, the Muslim population inside the land that would later become Israel was about **270,000–277,000**.

Step 2: Reconstructing the Migration Waves

We know that in 1922 there were about **277,000 Muslims** inside Israel's later borders. But who were they really? Were they descendants of an ancient "Palestinian" people — or the children of recent immigrants?

Historians answer this question by looking at the **migration waves of the 19th century.** The method is simple but solid: for each wave, we estimate the original influx, choose a midpoint year of settlement, and then apply a **1% net annual growth rate** — the rate universally accepted by scholars like **Justin McCarthy** and **Kemal Karpat** as the long-term demographic trend in Ottoman Palestine. This rate accounts for births, deaths, disease, and improvements in health over time.

With this tool in hand, let's walk through the migrations that reshaped Palestine.

Egyptians under Muhammad Ali (1831–1840)

In the 1830s, Egypt under **Muhammad Ali and his son Ibrahim Pasha** briefly occupied Palestine. To strengthen their control, they transferred thousands of Egyptians — soldiers, peasants, and conscription dodgers — into the land. Their presence is still visible today in village names like **Kafr Misr** ("Village of Egypt") and family names across the southern coastal plain.

- **Estimated influx:** 30,000–37,000
- **Midpoint year:** 1835
- **1922 descendants (87 yrs @1%):** ≈66,000–78,500

This was the **largest single wave** of Muslim migrants into Palestine.

Bedouin Tribes of Beersheba

By far the largest single Muslim group in southern Palestine were the nomad **Bedouin Tribes of the Negev and Beersheba**, counted at **72,900** in the 1922 census. The Ottomans and even British officials recognized them as **Najdi and Hejazi tribes**, who migrated from the **Arabian desert**.

- **Arrival period:** 18th–19th centuries (tribal migration from Arabia)
- **Estimated influx:** Continuous inflow, several tens of thousands
- **Midpoint year (for projection):** c. 1850
- **1922 size:** ≈72,900 (as recorded by the British census)

The Bedouin show how misleading modern claims of a "native majority" can be. The single largest bloc of Muslims inside Israel's 1967 borders in 1922 were not native Palestinians at all, but Arabian nomads transplanted from the deserts of the Hejaz and Najd (Arabian Peninsula).

Algerians after the French Conquest (1850s)

When France conquered Algeria, whole families fled to the Ottoman Empire. The sultan resettled thousands in Palestine, especially in the Galilee. Their communities became known as the **"Jaza'iri" villages**, preserving Algerian surnames to this day.

- **Estimated influx:** 3,000–3,500
- **Midpoint year:** 1855
- **1922 descendants (67 yrs @1%):** ≈6,800–7,800

Hauranis from Southern Syria (1850s–70s)

The fertile **Hauran region** of Syria suffered drought and instability in the mid-19th century, pushing thousands southward. Many settled in the **Jezreel Valley** and coastal plain. Some villages in Palestine still trace their ancestry to Haurani founders.

- **Estimated influx:** 8,000–10,000
- **Midpoint year:** 1860
- **1922 descendants (62 yrs @1%):** ≈15,600–19,500

Circassians & Chechens (1864–1870s)

Driven out by the Russian conquest of the Caucasus, Circassians and Chechens were resettled by the Ottomans in frontier zones. In Palestine, they built villages like **Kfar Kama** and **Rehaniya**. Their distinct culture and military loyalty made them a visible minority.

- **Estimated influx:** 800–900
- **Midpoint year:** 1865
- **1922 descendants (57 yrs @1%):** ≈1,500–1,800

Turkish Settlers (1850s–1890s)

The Ottoman state stationed thousands of officials, soldiers, and their families in Palestine. Many Turks stayed, marrying locally and embedding themselves in towns like Jerusalem, Jaffa, and Acre.

- **Estimated influx:** 3,500–4,000
- **Midpoint year:** 1865
- **1922 descendants:** ≈7,400–9,300

Balkan Refugees (Bosnians, 1878–1880s)

The Russo-Turkish wars pushed Muslim refugees out of Bosnia and the Balkans. Some were settled in Palestine, remembered locally as the **Bushnaq.** Their legacy survives in Galilee villages.

- **Estimated influx:** 1,300–1,500
- **Midpoint year:** 1880
- **1922 descendants (42 yrs @1%):** ≈2,600–3,500

Metawali (Shi'a from Lebanon, 1830s–40s)

Shi'a migrants known as the **Metawali** crossed from Lebanon and established villages in Upper Galilee. Their seven villages remained distinct well into the Mandate period.

- **Estimated influx:** 2,500–2,700
- **Midpoint year:** 1840
- **1922 descendants (82 yrs @1%):** ≈5,000–6,000

Maghrebis (North Africans, 1830s–40s)

Muslims from Morocco, Tunisia, and Libya (the **Maghrebis**) settled in Jerusalem's **Maghrebi Quarter** and coastal towns. They often came as pilgrims and stayed permanently.

- **Estimated influx:** 3,000–3,500
- **Midpoint year:** 1840
- **1922 descendants:** ≈6,200–7,350

Levantine Migrants (Lebanon/Syria, 19th century)

Not all migration came in dramatic waves. Thousands came steadily from Lebanon and Syria, drawn by citrus farming and jobs in port cities. These **Levantine migrants** blended into Palestinian towns but were well remembered as "newcomers."

- **Estimated influx:** 9,000–10,000
- **Midpoint year:** 1870
- **1922 descendants:** ≈18,500–22,200

Smaller Streams (Africans, Persians, Kurds, Yemenis, etc.)

Alongside these major groups were smaller flows — Africans (often ex-slaves or pilgrims), Persians, Kurds, Yemenis, and Central Asians. Though less visible, they still added up.

- **Estimated influx:** ≈2,500–2,700
- **1922 descendants:** ≈5,000–6,000

Internal Migrants from Gaza & West Bank

Finally, thousands of Arabs moved internally from the West Bank and Gaza into areas inside Israel's 1967 borders, especially Jaffa, Haifa, and the Sharon Plain.

- **Estimated 1922 total:** ≈15,000–30,000

The Grand Total

When all these groups are counted, their descendants inside Israel by 1922 numbered: ☞ **≈222,000–265,000 recent migrants**

Migration Ledger: Muslim Influx into Palestine (19th Century → 1922)

Migration Wave	Arrival Period	Estimated Influx	Midpoint Year	1922 Size (1% net growth)
Bedouin (Najdi/Hejazi tribes, Beersheba)	18th–19th c.	Tens of thousands	1850	72,900 (census 1922)
Egyptians (Muhammad Ali)	1831–1840	30,000–37,000	1835	66,000–78,500
Algerians (post-French conquest)	1850s	3,000–3,500	1855	6,800–7,800
Hauranis (southern Syria)	1850s–70s	8,000–10,000	1860	15,600–19,500
Circassians & Chechens	1864–1870s	800–900	1865	1,500–1,800
Turkish Officials & Families	1850s–1890s	3,500–4,000	1865	7,400–9,300
Bosnians/Balkan Muhacirs	1878–1880s	1,300–1,500	1880	2,600–3,500
Metawali (Shi'a, Lebanon)	1830s–40s	2,500–2,700	1840	5,000–6,000
Maghrebis (N. Africa)	1830s–40s	3,000–3,500	1840	6,200–7,350
Levantine Migrants (Lebanon/Syria)	19th century	9,000–10,000	1870	18,500–22,200
Smaller Streams (Africans, Persians, Kurds, Yemenis, etc.)	19th century	2,500–2,700	Various	5,000–6,000
Internal Migrants (from Gaza/West Bank)	Late 19th–early 20th	–	–	15,000–30,000

Step 3: Deducting the Migrant-Origin Descendants

We began with a **total of 277,000 Muslims inside Israel's pre-1967 borders in 1922**. That was the official census.

But as we showed in Step 2, the overwhelming majority of these were **descendants of 19th-century migration waves** — Egyptians brought by Muhammad Ali, Bedouin tribes streaming in from Arabia, Algerians fleeing the French, Hauranis from Syria, Turks and Bosnians planted by the Ottomans, and so on. When we apply a cautious 1% net growth rate to each wave, their 1922 descendants add up to between **222,000 and 265,000 people.**

Subtract those migrant-origin populations, and what are we left with? Not half a million "native Palestinians." Not hundreds of thousands of rooted peasants. Just **a thin residue of 12,000 to 55,000 Muslims** inside Israel's later borders in 1922 who can plausibly be called long-rooted to the soil.

Let that number sink in. A country of more than 10,000 square miles, and barely a few tens of thousands of truly "native" Muslims as of 1922.

> 1922 Muslims inside 1967 borders = ≈**277,000**
>
> Minus migrant-origin descendants = ≈**222,000–265,000**
>
> **Native residue (sedentary, long-rooted) =**
> ≈**12,000–55,000**

Step 4: Back-Projecting the Native Muslim Base to 1881

Having established the native Muslim residue in 1922, the next question is obvious: *what did that population look like at the eve of Zionist immigration — the First Aliyah in 1881?*

We know from Step 3 that the native sedentary Muslim population inside Israel's 1967 borders in 1922 was only ≈**12,000–55,000** people. To roll this number back four decades to 1881, we use the same demographic assumption employed by historians such as Justin McCarthy and Kemal Karpat: a **1% net annual growth rate** for Muslim populations in the late Ottoman period. This figure reflects high birthrates offset by high infant mortality, disease, famine, emigration and instability — in other words, realistic growth for a pre-modern society.

Over 41 years (1881 to 1922), a 1% annual growth rate multiplies a population by a factor of ≈**1.50**. To find the size of the native population in 1881, we simply reverse the formula:

Native (1881) = Native (1922) ÷ 1.50375

Applying this to the range:

- **Low estimate:** 12,000 in 1922 → ≈**8,000** in 1881.

- **High estimate:** 55,000 in 1922 → ≈**36,600** in 1881.

- **Midpoint:** 33,500 in 1922 → ≈**22,300** in 1881.

- Years between 1881–1922: **41**
- Native Muslims (1922): ≈**12,000–55,000**
- Native Muslims (1881): ≈**8,000–36,600**
- Midpoint: ≈**22,300**

This gives us a transparent estimate of the native Muslim population on the eve of Zionist immigration. Before comparing it with the Jewish community of the same period, we must first pause to recognize what these numbers alone reveal: in a land of more than 10,000 square miles, the truly long-rooted Muslim population in 1881 numbered only in the low tens of thousands.

Step 5: The Verdict — Jews vs. Native Muslims on the Eve of Zionism

We have now arrived at the decisive comparison. Numbers can be manipulated, myths repeated, slogans chanted — but the census evidence and careful demographic reconstruction leave us with hard facts.

By 1881, the eve of the First Aliyah, the **long-rooted native Muslim population inside the borders of Israel** (as they stood after 1967) was only ≈**8,000–36,600**, with a midpoint of ≈**22,300**.

What about the Jews? The so-called **Old Yishuv** — the established Jewish population in Jerusalem, Safed, Tiberias, and the smaller rural colonies — numbered **25,000–27,000** by the same year. These were not newcomers; they were Jews who had maintained a continuous presence in the land for centuries.

This finding strikes at the heart of the myth: the land was not home to a vast, ancient Arab nation. It was thinly populated, its Muslim inhabitants overwhelmingly descended from recent migrants, and **its truly long-rooted native Muslim base was smaller than the Jewish community** that had maintained continuous presence in the land for centuries.

Head-to-Head

Population	Size in 1881	Notes
Native Muslims	≈8,000–36,600 (midpoint ≈**22,300**)	Residue after deducting migrant-origin groups
Old Yishuv Jews	≈25,000–27,000 (midpoint ≈**26,000**)	Continuous Jewish presence + new arrivals

The Jury's Finding

On the eve of Zionist immigration, Jews were not a small minority intruding into a flourishing Arab country. The evidence shows that Jews **outnumbered or equaled the truly native Muslim population** inside the 1967 borders. The vast majority of Muslims then living in the land were descendants of **recent 19th-century immigrants** from Egypt, Syria, Arabia, Algeria, the Caucasus, and the Balkans.

This is the opposite of the modern myth. Far from Zionists displacing an ancient Arab nation, the record proves that Zionists returned to a land where the long-rooted Muslim population was smaller than the Jewish community itself — and where most of the so-called "Palestinians" were in fact the children and grandchildren of 19th-century migrants from Egypt, Syria, Arabia, and beyond.

Even Arab leaders have admitted this reality. Former Hamas Interior Minister **Fathi Hammad** confessed on Al-Hayat TV that "half of Palestinians are Egyptians and the other half are Saudis." The numbers show he was not exaggerating but stating a blunt truth: Palestine's Arab identity was overwhelmingly the product of recent migration, not ancient nativity.

Closing the Case on the "Desolate Land"

We have now examined the question from three angles — and the verdict is undeniable.

- **Exhibit A (Land Code):** By Ottoman law, nearly 80% of the land was classified as *mawat* — dead, uncultivated, and outside village boundaries. Only a tiny fraction was ever private freehold (*mulk*), and most of the rest was *miri*, owned by the Sultan. The myth of an ancient Arab peasantry clinging to ancestral farms collapses under the Ottomans' own definitions.

- **Exhibit B (Eyewitness Accounts):** From Mark Twain to Lamartine, from Oliphant to Thomson, travelers across centuries described Palestine as desolate — swamps, dunes, deserts, and a scattering of tents and huts. The land was not a bustling homeland of millions, but a neglected frontier where silence spoke louder than human presence.

- **Exhibit C (Census Reconstruction):** When we strip away 19th-century migrant inflows from Egypt, Syria, Arabia, Algeria, the Balkans, and the Caucasus, the 1922 census shows only ≈**8,000–36,600 long-rooted native Muslims** in 1881 — a population likely smaller than the Jewish Old Yishuv.

Taken together, the exhibits prove beyond reasonable doubt that the Zionist pioneers did not displace an indigenous nation. They returned to a land that was barren, sparsely populated, and whose Arab inhabitants were overwhelmingly recent arrivals.

But this is only the beginning of the story. To understand just how distorted the modern narrative has become, we must turn next to several critical topics.

- **Jewish Exodus During Ottoman Rule:** Long before Zionism, Jewish numbers in the land could have been far higher were it not for punitive taxes like the *jizya*, forced conversions, and discriminatory policies that drove many Jews into exile. Far from being dominant, Jews survived as a stubborn remnant under systemic oppression.

- **Healthcare Under Ottoman Rule:** If one wants to measure civilization by infrastructure, the contrast could not be sharper. By the late Ottoman period, Jews built and maintained the majority of hospitals in Palestine, while the Arab population had none of its own. Healthcare was provided almost entirely by Jewish institutions and, to a smaller degree, Christian missions. The Arab Muslim population contributed virtually nothing.

These are the next pieces of evidence we will examine. Each one deepens the case that the Zionist movement did not colonize a thriving land, but revived a desolate one — and that the real story of this land is Jewish endurance, return, and renewal against centuries of neglect and hostility.

Jewish Exodus During Ottoman Rule

While Ottoman Palestine saw an influx of Muslims during the Ottoman rule due to resettlement programs and migration, it simultaneously experienced an exodus of Jews. This departure was driven by a combination of economic hardships, systemic discrimination, and violent events that destabilized Jewish communities. Here are the primary causes behind this trend:

1. Heavy Taxation

The Ottoman Empire imposed discriminatory taxes on non-Muslims, including Jews and Christians. Two major taxes were particularly burdensome:

- **Jizya**: A head tax that non-Muslims had to pay simply for existing under Ottoman rule. This tax was both a financial strain and a symbol of subjugation.
- **Kharaj**: A land tax disproportionately targeting non-Muslim landowners, making it challenging for Jews to sustain agricultural livelihoods.

These taxes placed significant financial pressure on Jewish communities, forcing many to leave the region in search of better opportunities.

2. Restrictions on Employment

Non-Muslims faced restrictions on the types of jobs they could hold under Ottoman policies. Jews were barred from government positions, military roles, and many high-paying professions. They were often confined to small-scale trades, crafts, or moneylending, limiting their economic mobility and prospects for growth.

3. Episodes of Violence and Pogroms

Waves of violence targeted Jewish communities, further driving them from Palestine. Some notable incidents include:

- **1834 Hebron Massacre**: During an uprising against Egyptian rule, Jewish homes were looted, many residents were murdered, and others were left destitute.
- **1834 Safed Massacre**: Violent mobs ransacked Jewish homes, killed residents, and destroyed property.
- **1838 Hebron Massacre**: A devastating attack where Jewish synagogues and homes were destroyed, and lives were lost.

These episodes of violence left Jewish communities in a state of constant vulnerability, prompting many to flee for their safety.

4. Social and Legal Discrimination

As second-class citizens (*dhimmis*), Jews faced systemic discrimination under Ottoman rule. They were excluded from political representation and subjected to arbitrary treatment by local authorities. Such marginalization eroded their ability to thrive in the region.

5. Forced Labor

Although Jews were usually exempt from military conscription, they were often conscripted into forced labor by Ottoman authorities. This disrupted community life and imposed additional physical and economic burdens.

6. Jewish Expulsions During World War I

During World War I (1914–1918), the Jewish population in Palestine suffered severe losses due to Ottoman policies and wartime conditions. Thousands of Jews were expelled from cities like Tel Aviv and Jaffa by Ottoman authorities, who accused them of supporting the Allies.

Healthcare During Ottoman Rule

If you really want to understand why Palestine stayed sparsely populated under Ottoman rule, you have to look at health. Life expectancy was shockingly low — barely **35 to 40 years** on average — and infant mortality was among the worst in the world. In some areas, nearly one out of every three babies died before reaching their first birthday.

Epidemics were routine: **malaria, cholera, typhoid, trachoma**, and **dysentery** ravaged towns and villages every few years. With no sanitation system, no clean water supply, and no organized medical care, most people simply didn't survive long enough to grow families.

Hospitals were virtually nonexistent. By the early 20th century, the entire land of Palestine — from the Galilee to the Negev — had **fewer**

than 200 hospital beds in total. And almost **all of them were Jewish.** The rest of the country had almost nothing. In other words, there wasn't a single Arab-run hospital anywhere in the land.

The Jewish Foundations of Modern Healthcare

While the Ottoman authorities built little and maintained less, it was the Jewish community that introduced real healthcare to Palestine. These hospitals weren't just charitable projects — they were lifelines that kept the city alive.

- ✓ **Bikur Cholim Hospital**, founded in **1826**, was the first organized Jewish hospital in Jerusalem and one of the earliest in the entire Ottoman Empire outside Istanbul. It started with a few rooms in the Old City and treated Jews, Christians, and Muslims alike.

- ✓ **Rothschild Hospital**, established in **1854** through the support of the Rothschild family, offered free treatment to anyone who came through its doors. It quickly became one of the most respected institutions in Jerusalem.

- ✓ **Misgav Ladach**, founded in the **1850s**, served as a maternity and general hospital and later expanded as the city grew.

- ✓ **Shaare Zedek Hospital**, opened in **1902** on Jaffa Road, was the most modern facility in Ottoman Palestine. It had a pharmacy, surgery rooms, and trained physicians. Its Hebrew name — "Gates of Justice" — captured its mission: to heal all who needed care, regardless of religion.

These Jewish institutions formed the backbone of medical care in the country decades before Zionism. They were not built by governments, foreign missionaries, or colonial powers — they were built by the Jewish community itself.

The Missionary Hospitals — Few, Small, and with a Purpose

The only other hospitals in Ottoman Palestine were founded by European missionary societies. Their stated purpose was "to heal the body and save the soul" — meaning they offered free treatment in exchange for conversion. The **English Mission Hospital**, opened in **1844**, was the first of its kind. It had fewer than a dozen beds and openly advertised its mission to convert Jews. The **French St. Louis Hospital** (1851), **Russian Hospital** (1863), and **German Deaconess Hospital** (1890s) were similarly small, foreign-funded institutions aimed at Christian pilgrims and local converts — not at the Arab Muslim population.

Outside of Jerusalem, a few tiny missionary clinics existed — in **Nazareth**, **Tiberias**, and **Nablus** — each with no more than twenty beds. These were drops in the bucket compared to the vast, disease-ridden countryside that had no access to any medical facility at all.

The Arab and Ottoman Absence

It's important to stress what did not exist. The Ottoman authorities did not establish any meaningful healthcare system in Palestine, and there were no Arab or Muslim hospitals during the entire 400 years of Ottoman rule.

A Land Without Healing

By the eve of World War I, Palestine's total hospital capacity was still under 200 beds — and the overwhelming majority were Jewish-run. The rest belonged to small missionary clinics whose main goal was conversion, not medicine. The Arab Muslim population, by contrast, had no hospitals of their own and relied on traditional healers, herbal remedies, and prayer.

This lack of healthcare was not just a symptom of poverty — it was one of the reasons the land remained so thinly populated. Epidemics could wipe out entire families. Mothers often died in childbirth. Life expectancy barely touched forty. In the countryside, disease ruled and doctors were nowhere to be found.

Jewish institutions, on the other hand, had already begun modernizing medicine in Palestine decades before the First Aliyah. By the mid-19th century — while most of the region still lacked roads, schools, or sanitation — Jerusalem's Jewish community had already built hospitals like Bikur Cholim (1826), Rothschild (1854), and Misgav Ladach (1850s). These institutions were founded by Jews, served people of all faiths, and became the backbone of organized medical care in the Holy Land.

So when the Zionist pioneers arrived after 1881, they didn't invent healthcare in Palestine — they expanded what their predecessors had already built. The groundwork was there: Jewish compassion, Jewish philanthropy, and a belief that to heal the land, one must first heal its people.

Conclusion: The Myth of an Ancient Nation

The evidence from the Ottoman centuries paints a very different picture from the one repeated in modern political slogans. What the world came to call "Palestine" was not a unified country, nor was it home to an unbroken, ancient Arab nation. It was a sparsely populated frontier of a vast Islamic empire—a patchwork of villages, empty plains, and neglected valleys ruled from distant capitals.

Under Ottoman law, most of the territory was classified as *mawat*—dead land, unclaimed and uncultivated. The few settled areas were overwhelmingly state-owned *miri* land, not ancestral private property. There is no record, Ottoman or otherwise, of Zionists seizing land illegally. Every plot they acquired was bought, registered, and paid for.

33

Traveler after traveler—from Mark Twain to Laurence Oliphant—described Palestine as barren and desolate. Census records confirmed the same reality. Even by 1922, after decades of Ottoman resettlement policies and Arab immigration, fewer than 300,000 Muslims lived within what would later become Israel's 1967 borders. When those later migration waves are subtracted, the number of long-rooted Muslim families was smaller than the Jewish *Old Yishuv* that had endured in the land for centuries.

Jerusalem stood as the clearest example. From at least 1818 onward, every record—Ottoman, British, or European—showed a consistent Jewish majority. The city's demographic continuity belonged not to a fabricated "Palestinian" nation but to the Jewish people, who maintained an unbroken presence even through centuries of persecution, taxation, and exile.

For four hundred years of Ottoman rule, the land's story was one of neglect and transience. Populations shifted; empires rose and fell; the land lay mostly silent. Only the Jewish presence remained constant—small at times, but never extinguished.

The myth of an ancient, native Arab nation rooted in this soil collapses under the weight of these facts. The Ottomans themselves never recognized such a people; neither did the British who succeeded them. What they ruled was a province without a nation, a land awaiting revival.

When the Ottoman Empire fell in 1917, a new power stepped in—**Britain**. Under its rule, the land would awaken from centuries of neglect. The world would witness both a dramatic Jewish return and an equally dramatic influx of Arab migrants drawn by the opportunities that Jewish development created. What followed was not the birth of a "Palestinian nation," but a struggle over a land finally coming back to life.

Chapter 2
The British Rule (1917-1948)

When the Ottoman Empire collapsed after more than four centuries of rule, the Middle East was left without borders, governments, or national identities. Into that vacuum stepped the British and the French—two European powers eager to divide the spoils of a fallen empire.

The Artificial Creation of New Nations

The official British Mandate over Palestine began on **July 1, 1920**, but its roots go back to a secret wartime deal: the **Sykes–Picot Agreement of 1916**. This was an understanding between Britain and France to carve up the Ottoman territories into spheres of control. It had nothing to do with the people who lived there, their languages, their religions, or their histories. Western diplomats—sitting in offices thousands of miles away—drew lines on a map and in doing so, created countries that had never existed before.

From those lines emerged **Iraq, Syria, Lebanon, Transjordan**, and what became known as **Palestine**. These borders were artificial from the start, designed to serve imperial interests, not regional realities. The French wanted to secure their foothold along the Mediterranean; the British wanted to protect trade routes to India and access to the Suez Canal and Persian oil fields.

Transjordan, today's Jordan, was not a historic nation but a British creation—a buffer zone east of the Jordan River meant to stabilize Britain's new territories and protect the route from Cairo to Baghdad. Before 1920, this region was a stretch of tribal land under loose Ottoman control, inhabited by Bedouin clans and a few small villages. In 1921, the British installed **Emir Abdullah**, a Hashemite prince from Arabia, as ruler, giving birth to the new Emirate of Transjordan. Ironically, parts of what is now Jordan once belonged to the **ancient Kingdom of Israel**,

35

and even the name "Jordan" comes from the Hebrew word *Yarden*—"descend"—referring to the descent of the Jordan River.

Lebanon was another invention, molded by French colonial ambitions. In 1920, France redrew its borders to include the fertile Beqaa Valley and coastal Sunni towns, merging communities that had little shared identity: Maronite Christians, Sunni and Shia Muslims, and Druze. The name *Lebanon* itself derives from the Hebrew *Lavan*, meaning "white," a reference to the snowcapped mountains mentioned dozens of times in the Bible. The French saw Lebanon as a Christian enclave in a Muslim region—but the mix they created eventually produced a century of sectarian strife and civil wars.

Syria, too, was an artificial construction—an arbitrary union of diverse regions that had once been separate Ottoman provinces. French administrators cobbled together Damascus, Aleppo, and coastal Alawite territories into a single political unit, ignoring deep cultural and tribal divisions.

And then there was **Palestine**. Its borders were drawn not around a nation, but around a name—one that the **Romans had imposed almost 1,900 years earlier**. After crushing the Jewish revolt in 135 CE, the Romans destroyed the Second Temple, renamed Judea to *Provincia Palestina*, and expelled or enslaved much of the Jewish population. The name was borrowed from the long-extinct **Philistines**, a seafaring people who had vanished seven centuries before the Roman empire. Ironically, the word "Palestine" doesn't even exist in Arabic; because Arabic lacks the letter "P," it became *Falastin*.

By the early 20th century, *Palestine* was a label resurrected by European administrators, not a self-identified nation. It was simply the British term for the territory between the Mediterranean and the Jordan River. Under Ottoman rule, it had been nothing more than an administrative district centered around Jerusalem.

It's telling that **Jordan, Lebanon, Syria, and Iraq** all owe their modern existence to colonial mapmakers. They were political experiments built out of convenience, not continuity. Lebanon became a state in **1943**, Syria and Jordan in **1946**, and Iraq just a few years earlier. Each was a product of European design—a mosaic of tribes, sects, and minorities held together by external power.

This is why it's so ironic when critics of Israel claim that "Israel is a fake country created by the West in 1948." In reality, Israel is the only country in the region that **once existed in the same land, with the same name, language, and faith**, thousands of years before modern borders were even imagined. It is the one nation whose ancient roots run deeper than every state surrounding it.

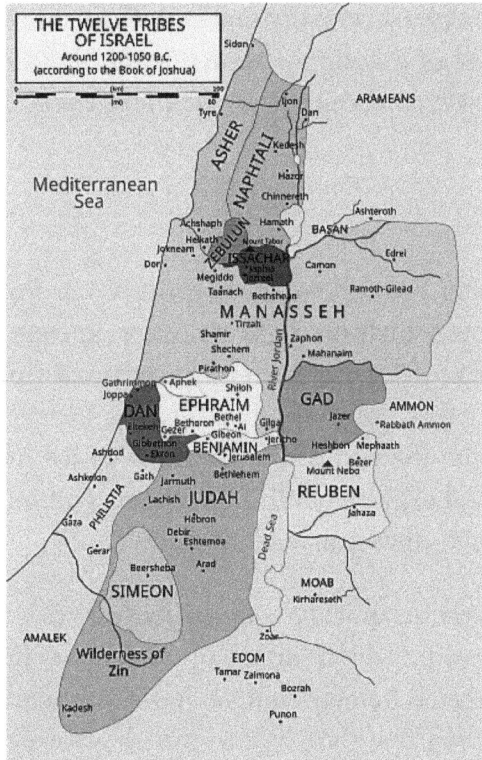

A map showing the territorial divisions of the 12 Tribes of Israel during biblical times.
Source: Wikimedia Commons / Public Domain

Here's another forgotten fact: the **original 1920 British Mandate for Palestine included Transjordan**—today's Jordan—within its borders. It was later split off to reward Emir Abdullah. So if modern activists insist that "Palestine must be freed," they might look eastward, where nearly 80% of the original Mandate territory already became an Arab state long before Israel was born.

The Balfour Declaration and the Betrayal of a Promise

While Britain was busy inventing new Arab states out of the Ottoman ruins, one promise it made was very different. In **1917**, at the height of World War I, Britain issued the **Balfour Declaration**, a 67-word statement that would change history:

> *"His Majesty's Government view with favour the establishment in Palestine of a national home for the Jewish people, and will use their best endeavours to facilitate the achievement of this object..."*

For the first time in two millennia, a world power formally recognized the Jewish people's historic right to their ancient homeland. The declaration, issued by Foreign Secretary **Arthur James Balfour**, was endorsed by the Allies, later approved by the League of Nations, and written directly into the text of the **British Mandate for Palestine**. It was not a colonial experiment; it was the recognition of an indigenous nation's revival in its ancestral land.

But this noble promise quickly collided with British imperial politics. Arab leaders across the region—many of them newly installed by Britain and France—protested fiercely against Jewish immigration and Zionist aspirations. Within a few short years, British officials began to retreat from their own commitments.

In 1921, Colonial Secretary **Winston Churchill**, facing unrest in the Arab world, drew a line down the middle of the Mandate and handed nearly 80 percent of it to Emir Abdullah as the new state of **Transjordan**. Jews were forbidden to settle east of the Jordan River. A year later, Churchill reassured Arab notables in Jerusalem that the Balfour Declaration "did not mean the imposition of a Jewish state" and that Britain had "no intention of making Palestine as Jewish as England is English.". It was the first in a long series of British reversals meant to placate Arab hostility, and it marked the beginning of a slow erosion of the Mandate's original purpose.

Throughout the 1920s and 1930s, Britain alternated between half-hearted support for Zionist development and outright obstruction. Arab riots were met with British inquiries that almost always concluded that Jewish immigration—not Arab violence—was the problem. Each new "White Paper" imposed tighter restrictions on Jewish land purchases and immigration.

The most infamous came in **1939**, on the eve of World War II. The **MacDonald White Paper** declared that Jewish immigration would be limited to **75,000** over five years—an average of only **15,000 per year**—after which it would require Arab consent. At the very moment when Europe's Jews were being hunted and murdered, the gates of their only refuge were closed. The same empire that had promised to facilitate a Jewish homeland now barred the survivors from reaching it.

What began as a declaration of moral vision in 1917 ended as an act of moral failure in 1939. Britain's shifting policies not only betrayed the spirit of the Mandate but also reshaped the demographic and political balance of the land for decades to come.

The First Census of Palestine

When the British took control of Palestine in 1918, they inherited a land that was still recovering from centuries of Ottoman neglect. Two years later, the **British Mandate** formally began, and in **1922**, the new administration carried out the first-ever comprehensive **census of Palestine**—a document that offers a rare, detailed snapshot of the region's population at the dawn of modern times.

This was not merely a bureaucratic exercise. It was a window into the real demographics of the land—recorded after **41 years of Zionist settlement**, when Jewish pioneers had already begun transforming swamps and deserts into farmland, introducing modern medicine, and revitalizing trade. The census, therefore, reflected both the modest population growth that Jewish development brought and the ongoing demographic shifts that would soon accelerate under British rule.

According to the 1922 census (Barron, *Census of Palestine 1922, General Tables*):

- **Muslims:** 590,890
- **Jews:** 83,794
- **Christians:** 73,024
- **Others:** 7,006 (Druze, Bahá'ís, Samaritans, etc.)
  Total population: approximately **755,000**

To grasp the scale, this entire land—from the Lebanese border to Beersheba—had fewer inhabitants than modern-day Jerusalem alone.

The city-level data reveal striking patterns:

- **Jerusalem**: 33,971 Jews and 13,413 Muslims — a **Jewish majority of almost 3:1**, confirming what earlier Ottoman records had already shown for decades.

- **Ramallah**: Now a center of Palestinian politics, it was in 1922 a Christian town of about 3,000 Christians and only 125 Muslims.

- **Bethlehem**: Also majority Christian, with 6,000 Christians and 800 Muslims — the complete reverse of today's demographics.

- **Tiberias**: Jews outnumbered Muslims **two to one**, continuing its long tradition as a center of Jewish life.

- **Jaffa** (later merged with Tel Aviv): Jews and Muslims were nearly equal in number, reflecting the area's growing prosperity and mixed population.

- **Haifa**: A small town where Muslims outnumbered Jews by roughly **3,000**, but both communities were still tiny by modern standards.

DISTRICT OF JERUSALEM—JAFFA						TABLE VII- POPUL
Locality.	Mohammedans			Jews		
	M.	F.	Total	M	F.	Total
JERUSALEM CITY :— Within the Walls	5,159	4,186	9,345	2,673	2,966	5,639
Without the Walls	2,645	1,423	4,068	14,040	14,292	28,332
Total	7,804	5,609	13,413	16,713	17,258	33,971

1922 British Census showing 33,971 Jews and 13,413 Muslims living in Jerusalem
Source: Archive.org, Public Domain.

Across the mandate of Palestine, towns that are today home to hundreds of thousands had **only a few thousand residents** a century ago. Much of the countryside remained empty or dotted with small hamlets, confirming what travelers like Mark Twain and Laurence Oliphant described decades earlier—a sparsely inhabited land waiting to be revived.

The census also tells a deeper story: the **Christian presence** that once dominated many historic towns was already shrinking, a decline that would continue under Arab nationalist pressure throughout the 20th century. By contrast, the **Jewish population**, though still a minority nationwide, was growing rapidly—driven by organized immigration, self-sustaining communities, and a vision to rebuild their ancestral homeland.

In short, the 1922 census marks a turning point: it captures the **moment when Ottoman stagnation gave way to revival**, when Jewish pioneers were reestablishing roots, and when the myth of an ancient, unified Arab "Palestine" began to crumble under documented facts.

Immigration and Transformation During the Mandate

The 1922 census captured a moment of transition — the beginning of dramatic change under British rule. Over the next two and a half decades, Palestine's population would expand rapidly, but not in the way modern narratives suggest. Both Jews and Arabs migrated in large numbers, yet their motivations and contributions were fundamentally different.

Jewish immigration was driven by a historic mission — the return to Zion, fueled by persecution in Europe and a desire to rebuild the Jewish homeland. Arab immigration, by contrast, was largely economic — drawn by the prosperity and jobs created by the Jewish revival of the land.

The Jewish return to Palestine did far more than alter demographics — it transformed the land itself. Within just a few decades, Jewish immigrants built the region's first modern economy and public infrastructure: draining malarial swamps, planting forests, constructing rail lines, and electrifying cities. Hebrew once again became a spoken national language, schools and universities were established, and entire towns such as Tel Aviv, Rishon LeZion, and Rehovot rose from barren sand dunes and rocky hills. The productivity of Jewish farms, factories, and ports turned Palestine from a neglected Ottoman backwater into one of the fastest-growing economies in the Middle East. This prosperity, in turn, attracted tens of thousands of Arab workers and families from neighboring lands—Egypt, Syria, Lebanon, and Transjordan—who came not out of political solidarity but for economic opportunity. The land was not being emptied; it was being revived—and that revival drew others to it.

Arab Immigration Under British Rule

When the British took over in 1920, they accelerated modernization by paving roads, expanding railways, building ports, and improving public health through vaccination campaigns. But the most significant demographic change came not from natural growth — it came from **migration**.

The Pull of Prosperity

British Palestine was booming. New industries — construction, agriculture, manufacturing, and services — offered wages far higher than those available in neighboring lands. The average income per person in Palestine reached **20–30 British pounds per year**, roughly **two to four times higher** than in Syria, Lebanon, or Transjordan. Arabs from these regions began streaming in to find work in Jewish-developed farms, citrus groves, and urban projects. The prosperity that Zionist enterprise created acted as a magnet for laborers seeking a better life.

The Push of Regional Turmoil

Beyond the economic lure, there was chaos to the north. In 1925, the **Great Syrian Revolt** erupted against French colonial rule. France responded with brutal aerial bombardments — including the leveling of entire districts of Damascus. Tens of thousands fled southward into British Palestine. Lebanon, also under French mandate, saw its share of violent clashes and instability, driving further migration into the more stable British-controlled territory.

The Burden of French Taxation

Economic pressure played its role too. French-ruled Syria and Lebanon imposed heavy taxes to fund their colonial military presence, with little reinvestment in local communities. In contrast, British taxation in Palestine was lighter and often directed toward improving trade routes, agriculture, and public services. The result was predictable: people voted with their feet, leaving French-ruled poverty for British-administered prosperity.

The Ease of Movement

Under British administration, **migration within British territories was virtually unrestricted**. People moved freely from Transjordan, Iraq, Egypt, and even Cyprus. And unlike Jewish immigrants from Europe — whose arrival was tightly controlled, documented, and often limited — Arab migrants faced almost no bureaucratic barriers.

The borders of Palestine stretched across more than **1,000 kilometers**, shared with Syria, Lebanon, Transjordan, and Egypt. Most of this frontier passed through remote deserts, mountain passes, and sparsely inhabited plains like the Sinai. There were **no fences, checkpoints, or patrol roads** — just open terrain. Arabs could simply walk across in small groups, settle in villages, and blend seamlessly with local populations who spoke the same language and practiced the same religion.

British officials knew illegal migration was happening but had neither the manpower nor the political will to stop it. Their limited resources were focused on policing ports, not patrolling deserts. As a result, tens of thousands of newcomers entered Palestine without record or restriction.

By the 1930s, this steady flow of undocumented migrants — Syrians, Lebanese, Egyptians, and Transjordanians — had **dramatically increased the Arab population** within the Mandate. Ironically, it was Jewish progress that made Palestine attractive. Zionists drained the swamps, built the roads, and created the jobs — and in doing so, unintentionally spurred the very Arab population growth that modern propaganda now portrays as "ancient and native."

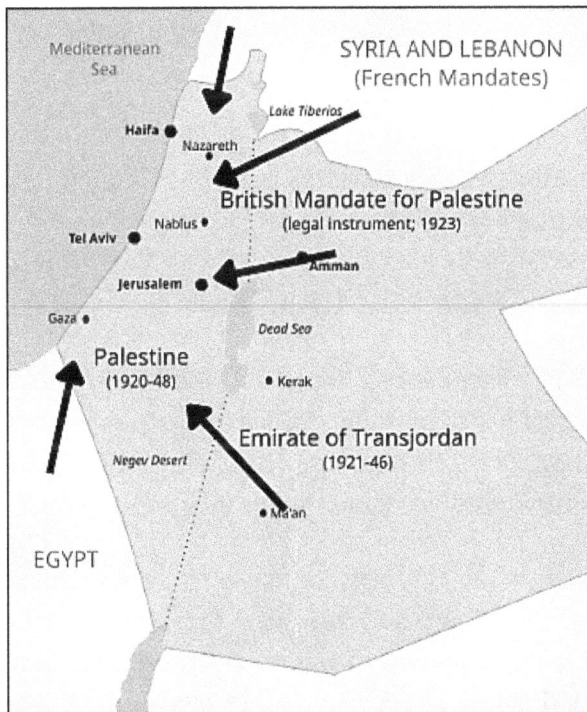

Arab Immigration by Land from Neighboring Regions

Arab vs. Jewish Immigration — The Hidden Demographic Story

Let's look at the numbers, not the slogans.

During the 1920s and 1930s, the **natural population growth rate of Palestinian Arabs averaged around 1% per year**. Life expectancy hovered between **35 and 40 years**, in stark contrast to today's 74+ years in the West Bank and Gaza. This low growth rate was typical for the Middle East under early 20th-century living conditions—high infant mortality, poor sanitation, and limited medical access.

Renowned historians such as **Justin McCarthy, Alexander Schölch, Kemal Karpat, Bernard Wasserstein, and Gad G. Gilbar**, working from Ottoman and British census data, have consistently placed Arab natural growth during this period in the **0.9%–1.2% range**—a consensus figure we can confidently use as a baseline.

Now let's compare the British censuses:

- **1922 census:** 590,890 Muslims in all of Palestine
- **1931 census:** 759,712 Muslims

That's an increase of **168,822 Muslims** over nine years.

If natural growth was roughly 1% annually, the Muslim population would have been expected to grow by **about 55,000** through births. The remaining **110,000–115,000 people** must therefore have come through **immigration**—documented or otherwise.

And that's just what the census *counted*. The British themselves acknowledged that they had no way to fully record cross-border movement. Because most Arab migrants entered on foot through the long, unguarded frontiers with **Syria, Transjordan, and Egypt**, the real number of newcomers was certainly higher—closer to **150,000 Arabs** by conservative estimates.

By contrast, **Jewish immigration between 1922 and 1931 totaled approximately 108,000** people. In other words, **Arab immigration during that same period equaled or surpassed Jewish immigration**—a striking reversal of the modern narrative.

The trend continued. By 1941, British administrative records listed **1,061,270 Muslims** in Palestine. Comparing this to the 1931 figure yields a rise of roughly **302,000 Muslims in a single decade**. Even accounting for natural growth (~77,000 at 1% per year), there remained an **"excess" of over 220,000 people**—a clear demographic signature of large-scale immigration from surrounding Arab territories. Including unregistered migrants, the real figure may have exceeded **300,000**. During that same decade, **Jewish immigration was ~242,000**.

These findings are not just theoretical—they're backed by meticulous research. Economist **Fred M. Gottheil**, in his landmark study *"The Smoking Gun: Arab Immigration into Palestine, 1922–1931"* (*Middle Eastern Studies*, Vol. 40, No. 4, 2004), analyzed British census data, agricultural records, and tax receipts from the Mandate period. His conclusion was unmistakable: **Arab population growth during the 1920s could not be explained by natural increase alone.**

Gottheil found that while birth and death rates could account for an increase of roughly **60,000–70,000 Arabs**, the actual recorded rise was more than **150,000**—leaving a surplus of **80,000–90,000** people that could only be explained by **unrecorded Arab immigration** from Syria, Lebanon, Transjordan, and Egypt. He demonstrated that this migration was directly tied to the economic expansion generated by Jewish agricultural, industrial, and infrastructural development.

In short, even academic analyses from outside the Zionist movement confirm what the historical record already makes clear: **the demographic surge among Arabs in British Palestine was not the result of deep-rooted nativeness, but of modern migration into a land revived by Jewish enterprise.**

So, who were the "colonizers"?

Pro-Palestinian narratives often claim that Israeli Jews should "go back to Europe," implying that Jews are foreign invaders while Palestinians are timeless natives. Yet the data tell the opposite story. Even today, **Ashkenazi (European) Jews make up barely 25% of Israel's population**. The majority—Mizrahi and Sephardi Jews—trace their roots to the Middle East and North Africa, regions from which they were expelled or fled during the 20th century.

If one insists on "going back," then perhaps the same logic should apply to the hundreds of thousands of Palestinians whose grandparents arrived from Syria, Lebanon, Egypt, and Transjordan during the British Mandate.

The numbers are unambiguous: **Arab immigration to Palestine during the early 20th century far exceeded natural growth and even surpassed Jewish immigration.**

The myth of "indigenous Palestinians versus foreign Jews" collapses under the weight of the historical record. What actually happened is simple: **Jews rebuilt a land that drew others in.** Prosperity created by Zionist revival—not ancient Arab settlement—explains the demographic explosion of the Mandate era.

The Natural Population Growth Myth

British officials were fully aware that large numbers of Arabs were entering Palestine illegally from surrounding territories during the Mandate years — and that they had neither the manpower nor the political will to stop it. With over a thousand kilometers of porous borders stretching across desert, mountains, and coastal plains, the British simply couldn't patrol every crossing. And in truth, many didn't want to.

Even official British reports admitted the problem. In the **Hope-Simpson Report of 1930**, commissioned after the 1929 Arab riots, Sir John Hope-Simpson devoted an entire section to what he called *"unrecorded immigration."* He wrote:

> *"Another serious feature of immigration is the number of persons who evade the frontier control and enter Palestine without formality of any kind. It is exceedingly difficult to maintain any effective control of the various frontiers of Palestine... The immigrant who wishes to evade the control naturally leaves the road before reaching the frontier and takes to the footpaths over the hills."*

He warned that these entrants "remain in the country" and that "no effective control of immigration... is possible unless steps are taken to deal with these irregular entrants." In other words, even the British themselves admitted they couldn't stop illegal immigration — nor fully count it.

Seven years later, the **Peel Commission (1937)** confirmed this reality, stating the need for *"an effective frontier organisation... for stopping smuggling, illegal immigration, and gun-running."* The Commission bluntly described "considerable difficulty" arising from uncontrolled migration, particularly from Syria and Transjordan, where economic hardship pushed Arab workers toward Palestine's growing economy.

One of the most revealing comments came from **C. S. Jarvis**, the British governor of Sinai (1923–1936), who noted that it was "very difficult to make a case out for the misery of the Arabs if at the same time their compatriots from adjoining States could not be kept from going in to share that misery." His firsthand observation — preserved in later British archives and cited by economist Fred Gottheil — shows that British administrators knew Arab migration into Palestine was steady and substantial.

British Officials Quietly Confirmed It

Other Mandate officials acknowledged the same pattern, even if discreetly. In 1931, **Lewis French**, the Director of Development for the British Administration, reported that "the prosperity of Palestine has resulted in considerable immigration of Arabs from neighboring countries." He specifically noted that many fellahin working the newly cultivated lands of the coastal plain had arrived "within recent years from the Hauran and from Transjordan."

The **A Survey of Palestine** (1946), an official government report prepared by the British for the United Nations, likewise admitted:

> *"The increase in the Arab population is partly due to natural increase and partly to immigration."*

It went further, acknowledging that

> *"the prosperity of Palestine has attracted large numbers of immigrants from neighboring Arab lands."*

Even outside government circles, historians and economists who later examined British archives reached the same conclusion. **Bernard Wasserstein**, in *The British in Palestine*, observed that

> *"Illegal immigration of Arabs into Palestine from neighboring lands was a recurrent concern of the Mandate authorities, though tolerated for economic reasons."*

The pattern was clear to all: Arabs from Egypt, Syria, Transjordan, and Lebanon flowed into Palestine seeking higher wages and better living conditions.

The "Natural Growth" Excuse

So why did the British still claim that the soaring Arab population was the result of "natural growth"? The answer was political convenience. By attributing the population surge to higher birth rates, British officials avoided drawing attention to their inability — or unwillingness — to enforce border control.

At times, British reports even suggested a staggering annual Arab growth rate of over 2 percent — more than double the 1 percent observed under Ottoman rule. Yet this explanation collapses under scrutiny:

1. **Rural Arabs had no access to healthcare.** Over 90% of Arabs lived in rural villages with no hospitals or clinics. Most medical facilities were concentrated in Jewish institutions in Jerusalem, Haifa, and Jaffa. Life expectancy remained around 35–40 years, virtually unchanged from the Ottoman period, and infant mortality rates were catastrophic.

2. **Vaccination campaigns barely reached the countryside.** The British launched limited urban vaccination drives, but these did little for the rural majority, who continued to battle malaria, typhoid, and dysentery.

3. **Census and birth records were unreliable.** Births and deaths in rural areas were almost never registered. Most births took place at home; deaths were followed by immediate burial. Illegal immigrants' children, however, were recorded as native-born, inflating the figures.

4. **No demographic model explains a sudden doubling of growth.** Historians like **Justin McCarthy**, **Kemal Karpat**, and **Alexander Schölch** agree that Arab natural growth during Ottoman rule averaged around 1% per year. There was no medical revolution in 1920 that could plausibly make that figure leap overnight.

5. **Even modern growth rates don't match the claim.** Today, with universal healthcare and sanitation, Palestinian population growth stands around 2–2.5%. It's implausible that an underdeveloped, malaria-infested society a century ago could have matched modern rates.

The Numbers Don't Lie

The myth of "natural growth" was a bureaucratic smokescreen. The British preferred to pretend that Palestine's Arab population had surged by itself rather than admit to uncontrolled illegal immigration — or to the fact that Zionist development had made the land a magnet for regional migrants.

The truth is simple: the Arab population in Palestine grew not because of an unprecedented baby boom, but because tens of thousands of Arabs from Syria, Lebanon, Transjordan, and Egypt crossed the border to share in the prosperity created by Jewish industry and labor. And the British, for political reasons, chose to look the other way.

Historical and Cultural Connections to the Land

There's a fundamental difference between **living in a land** and **belonging to it**. While Arabs migrated to Palestine during the late Ottoman and British Mandate periods mainly for economic reasons, the Jewish people's presence in the land of Israel is not a story of arrival — it's a story of return. Their cultural, linguistic, and spiritual identity was born here, shaped by the hills of Judea, the fields of Samaria, and the shores of the Galilee.

The Jewish Civilizational Continuity

Jewish connection to the land is not a modern political claim or a recent rediscovery. It's a **4,000-year-old historical continuum**, supported by archaeology, language, scripture, and living tradition.

The Hebrew Bible — one of the world's oldest and most widely read books — documents the formation of the ancient kingdoms of Israel and Judah, the building of the First and Second Temples in Jerusalem, and the exile and return of the Jewish people. But these aren't just religious traditions. Archaeology repeatedly confirms them.

Across Israel, excavations have revealed layers of Jewish life that stretch back millennia:

- The **City of David** excavation in Jerusalem has uncovered royal seals, administrative bullae, and inscriptions bearing names that appear in the Book of Kings.

- Ancient **Hebrew inscriptions** such as the Gezer Calendar, Siloam Inscription, and Ketef Hinnom amulets show the continuous use of the Hebrew language from the 10th century BCE onward.

- Hundreds of **synagogues** dating from the Second Temple and Byzantine periods have been found from the Galilee to the Negev, often with Hebrew and Aramaic inscriptions invoking God or blessing Israel.

- Coins minted by Jewish authorities — bearing names like "Yehud," "Shekel of Israel," and "Year Two of the Freedom of Israel" — testify to sovereign Jewish rule and a deep spiritual bond to the land.

These findings are so extensive that every archaeologist working in the region — Israeli, American, or European — acknowledges that the Jewish presence is **archaeologically dominant and uninterrupted** from antiquity through the modern era.

Ancient Jewish coins discovered during the archaeological excavation at Masada
Source: Jack1956 / Wikimedia Commons / CC BY 3.0.

Even after exile, Jewish communities never vanished from the land. A continuous Jewish population lived in cities like Jerusalem, Safed, Tiberias, and Hebron through Roman, Byzantine, Arab, Crusader, Ottoman, and British periods. Pilgrims, poets, and scholars from medieval Europe and North Africa described Jews praying at the Western Wall and tending communities in the Galilee.

In other words, the Jewish people did not "discover" their homeland in 1948 — they reestablished sovereignty in the same land where their ancestors had already built kingdoms, spoken their language, and prayed to their God.

The Absence of an Ancient "Palestinian" Civilization

By contrast, there is no evidence — archaeological, linguistic, or historical — of a distinct Arab "Palestinian" civilization predating the modern era. The term *Palestine* itself was a Roman invention, imposed in the 2nd century CE after Emperor Hadrian crushed the Bar Kokhba Revolt and renamed Judea as *"Syria Palaestina"* to erase Jewish identity from the map. The name was borrowed from the *Philistines* — a non-Arab, Aegean people who disappeared from history 1,200 years before Islam even existed.

When Arabs first arrived in the 7th century CE during the Muslim conquests, they did not create a new political or cultural entity called Palestine. Instead, the region was governed as a district within the broader empires of Damascus, Baghdad, Cairo, and later Constantinople. Throughout these centuries, the area that would later be called "Palestine" had no independent administration, no unique language, no distinct national identity, and no indigenous political institutions.

No coins, inscriptions, or artifacts exist that were ever minted by an "Arab Palestinian" state. The earliest coins and inscriptions in Arabic appear under the **Umayyad Caliphate**, headquartered not in Jerusalem but in Damascus. And even the Umayyads didn't refer to their territory as Palestine.

This historical silence is telling. The absence of archaeological or written evidence for an ancient Arab Palestinian culture underscores that Arab presence in the land was part of a wider Arab expansion, not a local or indigenous continuity.

Language, Faith, and Homeland

The difference between Jewish and Arab connections to the land is also cultural and linguistic.

The **Hebrew language**, first spoken over 3,000 years ago in the land of Israel, was the tongue of kings, prophets, and farmers. Even during centuries of exile, Jews preserved Hebrew as the sacred language of prayer and learning, ensuring that when they returned to their homeland, they could revive it as a living national language. Modern Hebrew, reborn in the late 19th century, is the only ancient language in the world to have been successfully restored to daily life — a feat possible only because the Jewish people had never severed their link to the land where it was born.

Arabic, by contrast, originated in the Arabian Peninsula, hundreds of miles away. It became the language of the Levant only after the 7th-century Islamic conquest. The Arabic spoken in Palestine today — a dialect of Levantine Arabic — developed as a result of cultural diffusion from Damascus, Aleppo, and Cairo, not from any ancient local linguistic heritage.

Religion follows a similar pattern. **Judaism** was born in this land. Its holiest sites — the Temple Mount, Hebron's Cave of the Patriarchs, Rachel's Tomb, the Galilee — all lie within the borders of ancient Israel. Every Jewish festival, prayer, and ritual is rooted in the geography of this land — from Passover in the spring harvest to Sukkot, which celebrates the ancient agricultural cycle of Canaan.

Islam, on the other hand, originated in Mecca and Medina, over a thousand kilometers to the south. While Jerusalem became Islam's third holiest city, its sanctity in Islam is derivative — rooted in its prior role in Judaism. Even the Al-Aqsa Mosque, constructed by the Umayyads in the 8th century, was built atop the ruins of the Jewish Temples, acknowledging a legacy that predated Islam itself.

Roots vs. Residence

This is the core difference: For the Jewish people, the land of Israel is the *cradle of their civilization.* For Arabs, Palestine was a *periphery of empire* — a frontier region that became populated mainly during the late Ottoman and British periods when new economic opportunities emerged.

The demographic record supports this distinction. By the time of the First Aliyah in 1881, most of the Muslim families living in the areas that later became Israel were themselves descendants of migrants from Egypt, Syria, the Hauran, or the Arabian Peninsula — groups who had settled only decades earlier under Ottoman relocation programs or in search of work. Their connection to the land was practical, not ancestral.

The Jewish people, by contrast, carried with them not only memories but texts, prayers, and rituals centered on this land. Every synagogue in the world faced Jerusalem. Every Passover Seder ended with the words, *"Next year in Jerusalem."* Every Jewish wedding concluded with the breaking of a glass and the vow, *"If I forget thee, O Jerusalem, let my right hand forget its skill."*

No other people has maintained such a continuous spiritual, linguistic, and cultural connection to the same homeland over such a vast span of time.

The Historical Verdict

Modern political debates often blur this distinction, framing the conflict as a struggle between two indigenous peoples. But history, archaeology, and culture all tell a different story. The Jewish connection to the land is **ancient, documented, and unbroken**. The Arab connection is **comparatively recent and migratory**, tied more to economic opportunity and imperial expansion than to deep-rooted heritage.

If we judge by history, language, religion, and archaeology — by the evidence carved into stone, written in scripture, and spoken in prayer — there is no comparison. The Jewish people did not come to someone else's land. They came home.

The British Mandate period was supposed to pave the way for a Jewish homeland. Instead, it became an era of restrictions, betrayals, and double standards. Britain, which had promised to support the establishment of a national home for the Jewish people, slowly turned from facilitator to obstacle. White Papers capped immigration even as Jews were being slaughtered in Europe, and British patrol boats turned away refugee ships packed with Holocaust survivors. Arab leaders, emboldened by British appeasement, unleashed waves of violence and riots, trying to halt the rebirth of a Jewish nation through terror and intimidation.

Yet while the British broke promises and the Arabs burned fields, the Jews built cities. They drained swamps, paved roads, and raised the first modern infrastructure the land had seen in centuries. Every act of discrimination was met with determination; every blockade, with self-reliance. Out of hardship came organization. Out of persecution came productivity.

By the 1930s, the Yishuv — the organized Jewish community — had created its own economy, health system, universities, and local government. It had banks, labor unions, power stations, farms, newspapers, and schools — a self-sufficient nation in everything but name. When the British finally left, they departed from a land the Jews had already transformed. Palestine under Ottoman rule had been a wasteland; under the Jews, it had become a living, breathing prototype of modern Israel.

And that is where the true story of national rebirth begins — not in declarations or diplomacy, but in seventy years of work, sacrifice, and vision.

Chapter 3

The Making of a Modern Jewish Homeland

When the first Zionist pioneers arrived in the late 19th century, the land of Palestine was a neglected, disease-ridden province on the outer edge of the decaying Ottoman Empire. It had no paved roads, no schools, few stone buildings outside Jerusalem, and vast stretches of swamp, desert, and barren hillsides. The population—scattered peasants, Bedouin tribes, and small Jewish communities in cities like Safed, Hebron, and Jerusalem—lived mostly from subsistence farming. Travelers described malaria-infested marshes, deforested hills stripped of topsoil, and a land that had literally been left to rot. What the world calls "colonialism" was, in fact, reclamation—the return of a people to their ancestral homeland to rebuild it from ruin.

For nearly **seventy years** before Israel's independence—between 1881 and 1948—the Jewish people transformed this wasted province into a modern society. They did not conquer; they created. They did not exploit; they revived. When neighboring Arab lands remained stagnant under feudal landlords and tribal rule, Jewish settlers introduced science, infrastructure, and civic institutions that would eventually form the foundation of the State of Israel. By the eve of independence, the Jewish Yishuv had built a functioning nation in every sense except name.

Agricultural Revival: Turning Swamps into Fields

The rebirth began with the soil. Early Zionist pioneers drained the malaria swamps of Hadera and the Jezreel Valley, cleared boulders from Galilee hillsides, and planted orchards where nothing had grown for centuries. Agronomists from Russia and Europe brought modern irrigation and crop-rotation methods unknown in Ottoman Palestine.

The **Jewish National Fund (JNF)**, established in 1901, became the economic and ecological engine of this transformation—redeeming

59

millions of dunams of land and planting more than **12 million trees**. What had been barren hills turned into forests and farmland, a literal greening of the desert.

Settlements such as Petah Tikva (1878), Rishon LeZion (1882), Zikhron Ya'akov (1882), and Rehovot (1890) became models of self-sustaining agriculture. By the 1930s, citrus exports from Jewish groves— particularly the world-famous Jaffa oranges—were supplying Europe, rivaling established Mediterranean producers. In less than two generations, the land that Mark Twain once called "a desolate country... given over wholly to weeds and thorns" was producing one of the most dynamic agricultural economies in the region.

Economic Foundations and National Institutions

Jewish development quickly expanded beyond agriculture into finance, energy, and industry. In 1902, the **Anglo-Palestine Bank** was established as the financial backbone of the Yishuv. It provided loans to farmers, merchants, and builders, funding new enterprises when no other credit existed. Decades later, it became **Bank Leumi**, Israel's national bank.

Anglo-Palestine Bank note, issued under British Mandate authority. Printed in English, Arabic, and Hebrew, it was issued by the Jewish-owned Anglo-Palestine Bank — later renamed Bank Leumi, Israel's national bank after independence.
Source: Arabmuslim12 / Wikimedia Commons / CC BY 3.0.

In 1923, engineer Pinhas Rutenberg founded the **Palestine Electric Corporation (PEC)**, constructing hydroelectric plants along the Jordan River and transmission lines that electrified towns and kibbutzim. For the first time in centuries, villages that had lived by oil lamp saw electric light.

The **Mekorot Water Company**, created in 1937, mapped aquifers, drilled wells, and built pipelines that carried life to the semi-arid Negev. These systems later became the backbone of Israel's national water network.

The Jewish construction firm **Solel Boneh (1924)** built roads, bridges, ports, and public buildings across the country. Its workforce—often new immigrants—literally laid the foundation of a modern state. Where Ottoman maps had only rough caravan trails, Solel Boneh paved highways linking Tel Aviv, Haifa, and Jerusalem.

In parallel, cooperatives such as **Tnuva (1926)** centralized food production and distribution, creating the region's first modern agricultural-marketing network. The same era saw the rise of **Palestine Cement**, **Palestine Potash**, and other Jewish industries that supplied building materials for the Yishuv's explosive growth.

Even in aviation, Jewish initiative led the way: **Palestine Airways (1934)** and **Aviron (1936)** pioneered civil flight training, setting the stage for both El Al and the Israeli Air Force. In culture, the **Palestine Symphony Orchestra (1936)**—founded by violinist Bronisław Huberman—brought together Jewish musicians fleeing Europe, later becoming the Israel Philharmonic.

Everywhere the word *"Palestine"* appeared on Jewish institutions— **Anglo-Palestine Bank**, **Palestine Electric Company**, **Palestine Cement**, **Palestine Symphony Orchestra**—proving beyond dispute that before 1948, *"Palestine"* was not an Arab national label but a geographic term proudly used by Jewish builders of the land.

Education and Intellectual Rebirth

Zionism understood that a nation could not be rebuilt without knowledge. In 1912, the **Technion – Israel Institute of Technology** opened in Haifa, the first modern engineering school in the Middle East. In 1918 came the **Hebrew University of Jerusalem**, formally inaugurated in 1925 on Mount Scopus. These institutions trained scientists, agronomists, and physicians who would lead Israel's post-1948 transformation into a scientific powerhouse.

Jewish schools spread across the Yishuv, teaching in revived Hebrew—a language reborn from the Bible into modern speech thanks to Eliezer Ben-Yehuda. By the 1930s, thousands of children were learning in Hebrew-medium schools, while adult education and vocational training centers equipped immigrants for farming, construction, and engineering.

Healthcare and Social Welfare

Long before independence, the Yishuv created one of the most advanced healthcare systems in the Middle East. The **Shaare Zedek Hospital** in Jerusalem (1902) and the **Hadassah Medical Organization** (1918) pioneered modern hospitals with sanitation, surgery, and obstetrics that served Jews, Arabs, and Christians alike. Hadassah nurses fought epidemics of malaria and trachoma that had ravaged Palestine for centuries.

In 1920, the Histadrut Labor Federation established **Kupat Holim Clalit**, a cooperative health fund providing affordable medical care for all workers—decades before Britain's National Health Service or America's Medicare. Mobile clinics and maternity wards reached even the smallest settlements. By the 1940s, infant mortality among Jews had dropped dramatically, and life expectancy had doubled compared to Ottoman times.

Urban Development and Infrastructure

The founding of **Tel Aviv (1909)** marked the rebirth of Jewish urban life. What began as 66 families dividing sand dunes outside Jaffa became a thriving modern city with paved streets, electric lights, and a Hebrew-speaking population. Architects designed it in Bauhaus style, earning later recognition as the "White City." By the 1930s, Tel Aviv had its own port, university, theaters, and newspapers—a living symbol of Jewish renewal.

Elsewhere, the Yishuv built new towns like Ramat Gan, Herzliya, and Netanya. Roads and railways connected distant settlements; pipelines brought water to the Negev. While neighboring Arab towns still relied on donkeys and wells, Jewish areas had buses, power grids, and telephones. The contrast was so visible that Arabs from neighboring lands began migrating for work—drawn by the prosperity Jews had created.

Electricity, sanitation, and urban planning replaced centuries of neglect. British observers even admitted that "no other people under the Mandate have contributed so much to the country's progress as the Jews." By the late 1930s, Jewish enterprise accounted for 80 percent of all public works in Palestine.

Culture, Labor, and Community

Material progress alone did not define the Jewish renaissance; spirit did. The **Histadrut (1920)** united workers across industries, promoting solidarity and self-reliance. Its subsidiaries, such as **Solel Boneh**, became symbols of the working Zionist ethos—Jews building their homeland with their own hands.

The Yishuv fostered vibrant cultural life: Hebrew newspapers, publishing houses, theaters, and youth movements like Hashomer Hatzair and Betar. The arts flourished—painters like Reuven Rubin, poets like Chaim Nachman Bialik, and musicians from Europe found a home in a land finally stirring back to life.

A Nation in Everything but Name

By 1939, the Jewish Yishuv governed itself through elected institutions— the **Jewish Agency**, **Vaad Leumi**, and **Knesset Yisrael**— functioning as a proto-government. It ran its own courts, police, health system, schools, and defense organizations such as the **Haganah**. In contrast to Ottoman inertia and British mismanagement, the Jews built from nothing a cohesive society rooted in democracy, equality, and collective responsibility.

Neighboring Arab countries, still mired in illiteracy, tribalism, and feudal dependency, looked almost medieval by comparison. While Cairo and Damascus debated ideology, Tel Aviv was exporting citrus, manufacturing textiles, and opening cinemas. The modernization of Palestine was not imported by empire—it was built by Jews who believed work itself was holy.

Jewish pioneers, "Biluim", in Migdal, Ottoman Palestine, 1880's
Source: Wikimedia Commons / Public Domain

Major Jewish Institutions and Achievements in Pre-State Israel (1878–1948)

Year Founded	Institution / Project	Field / Sector	Key Contribution
1878	Petah Tikva	Agriculture	First modern Jewish farming colony; "Mother of Settlements."
1882	Rishon LeZion	Agriculture	Early Zionist settlement; introduced modern irrigation and vineyards.
1882	Zikhron Ya'akov	Agriculture	One of the first Baron Rothschild-sponsored colonies.
1901	Jewish National Fund (JNF)	Land Reclamation / Ecology	Redeemed millions of dunams of land; planted over 12 million trees.
1902	Shaare Zedek Hospital (Jerusalem)	Healthcare	First modern hospital in Jerusalem; served Jews, Muslims, and Christians.
1902	Anglo-Palestine Bank	Finance	Provided capital to Jewish farmers and builders; later became Bank Leumi, Israel's national bank.
1909	Tel Aviv	Urban Development	First modern Hebrew-speaking city; symbol of Zionist urban renewal.

1912	Technion – Israel Institute of Technology (Haifa)	Education / Science	First technical university in the Middle East; trained engineers and scientists.
1918	Hebrew University of Jerusalem	Higher Education	First modern university in Palestine; cornerstone of Israel's academic life.
1918	Hadassah Medical Organization	Healthcare	Established modern hospitals and clinics; reduced disease and infant mortality.
1920	Histadrut (General Federation of Labor)	Labor / Social Welfare	Organized workers, created cooperatives, and founded nationwide healthcare (Kupat Holim Clalit).
1923	Palestine Electric Corporation	Infrastructure / Energy	Electrified Palestine; founded by engineer Pinhas Rutenberg.
1924	Solel Boneh Construction Company	Infrastructure / Labor	Built roads, ports, and bridges; symbol of Jewish self-reliance.
1926	Tnuva Cooperative	Agriculture / Industry	Unified food production and distribution; ensured food security.
1934	Palestine Airways	Aviation / Transport	First Jewish airline in the region; precursor to El Al.

1936	Palestine Symphony Orchestra	Culture	Founded by Bronisław Huberman; evolved into the Israel Philharmonic.
1937	Mekorot Water Company	Infrastructure / Engineering	Built pipelines and wells; foundation of Israel's national water system.
1939	Tel Aviv Port	Trade / Infrastructure	Established first Jewish-built port; bypassed restrictive British control.

Conclusion: The Rebirth Before the State

By the time Israel declared independence in 1948, the transformation was complete. A land once derelict under centuries of Ottoman neglect had become a thriving modern society with banks, universities, hospitals, roads, electricity, and agriculture. In just two generations, Jewish pioneers had done what no empire had achieved: they revived a land and reawakened a nation.

This was not colonization—it was restoration. It was the return of a people to their ancestral home, rebuilding its soil, language, and soul. Long before statehood, the Jewish nation already existed—in its fields, its schools, its laboratories, and its spirit. Israel in 1948 was not born from politics, but from seventy years of labor, faith, and rebirth.

Chapter 4

Jerusalem: Myths, Claims, and Realities

Jerusalem is deeply significant to Judaism, Christianity, and Islam. For Jews, it is the holiest city, home to the Temple Mount and the ancient First and Second Temples. For Christians, it is where Jesus was crucified, buried, and resurrected, central to their faith. In Islam, it is revered as the site of **Al-Aqsa Mosque** where Muslims believe that the Prophet Muhammad's ascension to heaven during the Night Journey occurred.

The Palestinian demand from Israel revolves around the liberation of Al-Aqsa Mosque from what they view as Jewish encroachment and control over the sacred site. Many Palestinians perceive visits by Jewish groups of the Temple Mount/Al-Aqsa compound as attempts to alter the status of the area as a Muslim holy site.

The Muslim world's support for Palestinians is significantly driven by the centrality of Al-Aqsa Mosque to Islamic identity. Many Muslim countries and organizations see the Palestinian struggle as inseparable from the protection and preservation of Al-Aqsa. The defense of Al-Aqsa resonates deeply across the Muslim world, uniting diverse political and ideological groups in their advocacy for Palestinians. This shared religious bond amplifies solidarity with Palestinians, framing their cause as not only a political struggle but also a collective duty to safeguard one of Islam's holiest sites.

Across the Muslim world, a powerful narrative took hold — that Jerusalem is Muslim, and Jews are foreign intruders. Yet history tells a very different story. Long before Israel's founding, and even before modern Zionism, **Jews were not outsiders in Jerusalem but its largest and most enduring community.** The city's Jewish presence isn't a product of politics or conquest — it's a continuation of millennia of life, worship, and heritage rooted in the very heart of Jerusalem.

A City with a Jewish Majority Long Before Zionism

Historical evidence shows that Jews constituted the largest population group in Jerusalem for more than a century before the establishment of the State of Israel and the rise of Zionism. This majority is not a modern development but a well-documented fact supported by travelers, consuls, and official censuses throughout the Ottoman period.

1818 – Dr. Robert Richardson

Dr. Robert Richardson, family physician to the Earl of Belmore, visited Jerusalem in 1818 and observed that the Jewish population was roughly twice that of the Muslims, estimating about **10,000 Jews, 5,000 Muslims, and around 4,000 Christians**. His account is one of the earliest recorded descriptions of a Jewish plurality in the city.

1844 – Ottoman Census and the Prussian Consul Ernst-Gustav Schultz

The first Ottoman census of Jerusalem, confirmed by Prussian Consul **Ernst-Gustav Schultz** and later cited in *Encyclopaedia Britannica* (1853), recorded **7,120 Jews, 5,000 Muslims, and 3,390 Christians.** This official count provides the first administrative evidence that Jews were already the largest group in the city.

1846 – Titus Tobler (Swiss Explorer)

Swiss physician and explorer **Titus Tobler** published detailed figures listing **7,515 Jews, 6,100 Muslims, and 3,558 Christians**. His numbers align closely with the Ottoman census and Schultz's report, confirming a sustained Jewish plurality.

1850s–1860s – British Consular Reports

British officials stationed in Jerusalem noted the steady growth of the Jewish population and the stagnation or decline of Muslim numbers.

- **1853 – James Finn**, British Consul in Jerusalem, described Jews as forming "the greater part of the population."
- **1864 – British Consular Dispatches**, summarized in later demographic studies, reported roughly **8,000 Jews to about 5,000 Muslims and 5,000 Christians**, confirming the same ratios later published in travel guides.

1866 – John Murray Travel Guide

The John Murray Handbook for Travellers in Syria and Palestine (3rd edition, 1866) reported similar proportions: 8,000 Jews, 4,000 Christians, and 4,000 Muslims. This widely circulated guidebook for European visitors reflected on-the-ground realities in Jerusalem at the time, noting that Jews had become the city's dominant community.

1874 – British Consul W.H. Young

By 1874, British Consul **W. H. Young** reported approximately **10,000 Jews, 5,000 Muslims, and 5,000 Christians**, showing that Jerusalem's Jewish majority had become a long-term demographic feature.

1896 – Vital Cuinet and the Calendar of Palestine (5656)

The French geographer **Vital Cuinet** recorded that Jews were by far the largest community in Jerusalem. The *Calendar of Palestine* for that same year lists **28,112 Jews, 8,560 Muslims, and 8,748 Christians**, giving Jews more than a two-to-one majority.

1922 – British Mandate Census

At the close of Ottoman rule and the start of the British Mandate, the **1922 census** documented **33,971 Jews and 13,413 Muslims** within Jerusalem's municipal limits—nearly a **three-to-one Jewish majority**.

From Dr. Richardson's 1818 observations through the British census of 1922, every major record—official, consular, and academic—confirms the same demographic reality: Jews constituted the largest population group in Jerusalem throughout the 19th century and into the early 20th. This continuity of majority status is a matter of historical record, established long before modern political movements or statehood.

In short, Jerusalem was a Jewish-majority city under both Ottoman and British rule, decades before Zionism — a historical reality often forgotten in today's debates.

Year	Source / Observer	Jews	Muslims	Key Notes
1818	Robert Richardson (Family Doctor to the Earl of Belmore)	~10,000	~5,000	One of the earliest records of a Jewish plurality in the city.
1844	Ernst-Gustav Schultz, Prussian Consul (as cited in *Encyclopaedia Britannica*, 1853)	7,120	5,000	First Ottoman census of Jerusalem — Jews already the largest group.
1846	Titus Tobler (Swiss explorer)	7,515	6,100	Tobler confirmed a clear Jewish majority.

1864	British Consulate (Jerusalem Report)	8,000	4,500	Reinforces the steady Jewish lead.
1866	*John Murray Travel Guide*	8,000	4,000	Confirms Jews as the largest community.
1874	W. H. Young, British Consul	10,000	5,000	Official British record — Jewish population double any other group.
1896	Vital Cuinet (*La Turquie d'Asie*)	Jews noted as dominant group	–	French geographer affirmed Jewish numerical dominance.
1896 (alt. source)	*Calendar of Palestine for the Year 5656*	28,112	8,560	Late-Ottoman data showing Jews forming ~60% of the city's population.
1905	Ottoman Census of Jerusalem District	45,000	12,000	Within the district (Old City + surroundings), Jews outnumbered Muslims 3 : 1.
1922	British Mandate Census	33,971	13,413	Confirms that Jews remained the majority entering the British Mandate era.

Despite this well-documented history, groups like Hamas have built their ideology on denying it. They replace centuries of Jewish presence with a narrative of exclusivity, using religion as a political weapon. In their hands, Jerusalem's holiest sites become tools for incitement rather than places of faith.

Hamas's Weaponization of Al-Aqsa

For Hamas, Al-Aqsa isn't just a mosque—it's a weapon. The group has turned a sacred place into a tool for spreading hate and fueling conflict. Rather than protecting faith, Hamas uses religion as a shield and a sword — a tool to inflame emotions, recruit followers, and justify acts of terror under the banner of defending Islam's third holiest site.

*The **official Hamas emblem** shows two crossed swords in front of the Al Aqsa Mosque in Jerusalem. The mosque is framed by two Palestinian flags with the phrases in Arabic: "No god, but Allah" and "Muhammad is the prophet of Allah". Source: Wikimedia Commons – "Emblem of Hamas,"*

In Islamic belief, Al-Aqsa carries great significance as the place associated with the Prophet Muhammad's Night Journey and ascension to heaven. This symbolism gives the site enormous power in the hearts of Muslims worldwide — and Hamas knows it. The organization exploits that devotion to turn a local political struggle into a religious one, claiming that any Jewish presence on or near the Temple Mount is a desecration of Islam itself. Every Jewish visitor, every Israeli security patrol, every archaeological dig is framed as an attack on Al-Aqsa — a call to jihad.

This is not about theology. It's about control. By invoking Al-Aqsa, Hamas taps into deep religious emotions that transcend borders. Millions of Muslims who might otherwise have little connection to the Israeli-Palestinian conflict are drawn into Hamas's narrative through this religious trigger. The slogan *"Al-Aqsa is in danger"* has become one of the group's most effective propaganda tools — repeated in mosques, classrooms, and media across the Muslim world.

The result is a manufactured sense of holy urgency. Hamas tells its followers that violence against Jews is not only political resistance but divine duty. The group's charter explicitly defines its war as a *religious obligation* — a sacred mission to "liberate" all of Palestine in the name of Al-Aqsa. When Hamas launched its massacre on October 7, 2023, it named it **"Operation Al-Aqsa Flood,"** claiming to avenge supposed "desecrations" of the mosque. In truth, there was no attack on Al-Aqsa — only a calculated exploitation of faith to justify atrocities.

By turning a spiritual symbol into a tool of violence, Hamas has desecrated the very religion it claims to defend. Its obsession with Al-Aqsa is not about prayer or piety — it's about power. And in doing so, Hamas has ensured that what should be a house of worship remains one of the world's most dangerous flashpoints.

Does Islam Really Have a Claim to Jerusalem?

The historical and theological context of the Al-Aqsa Mosque's establishment in Jerusalem points to a <u>deliberate effort to assert Islamic dominance over Judaism and Christianity</u>, especially by placing it on the Temple Mount, the site where the Jewish Temples once stood.

One key argument questioning the sanctity of Al-Aqsa in Islam is the fact that Jerusalem is not mentioned in the Quran. The term "al-Aqsa" (meaning "the farthest mosque") appears only once, in Surah Al-Isra (17:1), which describes the Prophet Muhammad's Night Journey (Isra) from the "Sacred Mosque" (Kaaba in Mecca) to the "farthest mosque." However, the Quran does not explicitly link the "farthest mosque" to Jerusalem. At the time of this revelation, no mosque existed in Jerusalem; the city was under Byzantine Christian rule, and the Temple Mount was in ruins.

Islamic tradition later associated the term "al-Aqsa" with Jerusalem, but this connection emerged decades after Muhammad's death, during the **Umayyad Caliphate**. This retroactive linkage raises questions about whether the identification of Al-Aqsa with Jerusalem was a theological construct rather than an inherent Islamic belief.

The construction of Al-Aqsa Mosque in its current location was initiated by the Umayyad Caliph Abd al-Malik in the late 7th century CE. This period was marked by intense rivalry between Islam, Christianity, and Judaism. By building Al-Aqsa on the Temple Mount—traditionally the site of the First and Second Jewish Temples—the Umayyads effectively appropriated a location deeply revered in Jewish tradition.

This act served several purposes:

1. **Religious Supremacy**: Building a major Islamic site on the Temple Mount allowed the Umayyads to assert Islam's dominance over Judaism and Christianity.

2. **Political Legitimacy**: Choosing Jerusalem, a city deeply significant to Jews and Christians, helped the Umayyad caliphs solidify their authority and bolster their claim as leaders of the Islamic world.

3. **Theological Symbolism**: Placing Al-Aqsa on the Temple Mount effectively erased the Jewish connection to the site, reframing it as exclusively Islamic.

The phrase "al-Aqsa" itself is ambiguous and can be interpreted as referring to any distant location. Before the Umayyads associated it with Jerusalem, early Islamic traditions and scholars suggested various interpretations of the term. Some linked it to sites in Arabia or other parts of the Middle East. This theological flexibility suggests that the association of "al-Aqsa" with Jerusalem was not divinely mandated but rather a human decision motivated by political and religious considerations.

Hijacking Jewish and Christian History

Early Islamic traditions placed no emphasis on Jerusalem, which sharply contrasts with the city's central role in Judaism and Christianity. For Jews, the Temple Mount is the holiest site, home to the First and Second Temples. For Christians, Jerusalem holds immense significance as the site of Jesus' crucifixion and resurrection. By claiming the Temple Mount, the Umayyads aimed to overshadow these traditions and position Islam as the ultimate fulfillment of the Abrahamic faiths.

The intentional construction of Al-Aqsa on the Temple Mount carries significant implications for interfaith relations and historical narratives. It was an effort to overshadow the Jewish and Christian heritage of Jerusalem, redefining it with an Islamic identity.

Furthermore, the lack of Quranic evidence for Jerusalem's significance to Islam challenges the theological justification for the site's sanctity.

While later Islamic traditions sought to elevate Jerusalem's status, these efforts appear to have been driven by political agendas rather than authentic religious doctrine.

Erasing the Jewish Legacy of the Temple Mount

While Jerusalem is not mentioned even once in the Quran, it is mentioned over 600 times in the Jewish Bible.

Jerusalem holds unparalleled importance in Judaism, serving as the spiritual and historical heart of the Jewish faith. It is home to the Temple Mount (Har HaBayit), the site of the First and Second Temples, which were central to Jewish worship and the focus of religious practice for centuries. According to Jewish tradition, the Temple Mount is where Abraham prepared to sacrifice his son Isaac, demonstrating unwavering faith in God. Often referred to as Zion, Jerusalem represents the deep and unbreakable connection between the Jewish people and their homeland. Jews around the world pray facing Jerusalem, and their prayers and rituals reflect a constant hope for the rebuilding of the Temple and a return to Zion.

Jerusalem is also the focal point of Jewish identity and longing, especially during periods of exile. After the destruction of the Second Temple in 70 CE by the Romans, Jews around the world continued to express their deep attachment to Jerusalem through rituals and traditions, such as breaking a glass at weddings to commemorate the loss of the Temple and ending the Passover Seder with the words, *"Next year in Jerusalem."* Even when scattered across continents, Jerusalem remained the compass of Jewish prayer, art, and poetry—a symbol of hope and divine restoration.

This unwavering devotion survived through centuries of persecution and exile. While empires rose and fell, the Jewish people kept Jerusalem alive in their daily prayers and their dreams. It was not merely a city on a map but the beating heart of Jewish faith, history, and nationhood. No other people have maintained such a continuous spiritual and cultural bond to one city for over three millennia.

The Arch of Titus in Rome features a detailed relief depicting Roman soldiers carrying the Menorah from the Second Temple in Jerusalem after its destruction
Source: Steerpike / Wikimedia Commons / CC BY 3.0.

Archaeological Evidence Supports Jewish Roots, Not Arab Claims

Jewish archaeological findings provide overwhelming evidence of the deep and continuous historical roots of the Jewish people in Jerusalem. Layer after layer of the city's soil tells the same story: this was the ancient heart of the Jewish nation. Excavations throughout Jerusalem—especially in the City of David, the Western Wall tunnels, and the Ophel area south of the Temple Mount—have uncovered artifacts directly confirming the city's central role in biblical-era Jewish civilization.

Among the most remarkable discoveries are **inscriptions in ancient Hebrew**, royal seals bearing the names of officials mentioned in the Bible, and thousands of coins minted during both the First and Second Temple periods. These coins often bear inscriptions such as *"For the Freedom of Zion"* and *"Jerusalem the Holy"*, offering tangible proof of

Jewish sovereignty and identity long before the rise of Christianity or Islam. Archaeologists have also unearthed pottery fragments, ritual baths (mikva'ot), oil lamps, and household items that reveal a thriving and literate urban society built around Temple worship and Jewish law.

Prominent architectural findings leave little doubt about the depth of Jewish civilization in Jerusalem. The **Hezekiah Tunnel**, carved through solid rock in the late 8th century BCE, stands as a masterpiece of ancient engineering—built by King Hezekiah to secure Jerusalem's water supply during the Assyrian siege described in the Book of Kings. The discovery of the **Siloam Inscription**, carved into the tunnel's wall, provides one of the oldest known Hebrew texts, confirming both the Bible's historical narrative and the technological sophistication of the kingdom of Judah.

Equally significant are the **Dead Sea Scrolls**, discovered in the Qumran caves near the Dead Sea between 1947 and 1956. Written between the 3rd century BCE and the 1st century CE, these scrolls include biblical manuscripts, prayers, and legal writings that illuminate Jewish life during the Second Temple period. They bridge the world of ancient Israel and modern Judaism, preserving the very scriptures that continue to define Jewish faith today.

And then there is the **Western Wall**, the surviving outer structure of the Second Temple complex built by King Herod around 19 BCE. For nearly two thousand years, Jews from across the world have turned toward this wall in prayer, mourning the loss of the Temple and yearning for Jerusalem's restoration. Its stones bear the marks of time and devotion—each layer representing an unbroken chain of worship and memory.

*The **Great Isaiah Scroll**, one of the **Dead Sea Scrolls** discovered in the Qumran Caves near the Dead Sea, dating from around the 2nd century BCE. Written in ancient Hebrew, it is the oldest complete copy of a biblical book ever found — powerful evidence of the deep Jewish presence, literacy, and spiritual life in the Land of Israel long before the rise of Islam or Arabic culture.*
Source: Public Domain via Wikimedia Commons.

In contrast, there is no archaeological evidence of an ancient "Arab Palestinian" civilization in Jerusalem or anywhere in the land corresponding to modern Israel. No coins, inscriptions, or cultural artifacts exist that indicate the presence of a distinct Arab Palestinian identity in antiquity. The Arab presence in the region began centuries later, following the Islamic conquests of the 7th century CE, when Arabic language and Islamic culture spread from the Arabian Peninsula across the Levant.

Archaeology doesn't serve ideology—it serves truth. And the truth, written in stone, clay, and parchment, is clear: Jewish life and worship in Jerusalem are as ancient as the city itself. Every discovery reinforces the same reality — that Jerusalem was, and has always been, the center of Jewish civilization.

The West's Hypocrisy on Jerusalem

One of the most glaring inconsistencies in global politics is the refusal of most Western nations, aside from the United States, to recognize Jerusalem as the capital of Israel. Despite the city's millennia-old significance as the spiritual and historical heart of Judaism and its clear Jewish majority since at least the 18th century, many Western governments continue to treat Jerusalem as a "disputed" city. This refusal disregards both historical facts and Israel's legitimate right, as a sovereign nation, to designate its own capital.

In contrast to the wavering stance of other Western nations, the United States boldly recognized Jerusalem as the capital of Israel on December 6, 2017. The U.S. also relocated its embassy from Tel Aviv to Jerusalem on May 14, 2018.

The refusal to recognize Jerusalem as Israel's capital is especially puzzling given the city's overwhelming Jewish identity and history. For over three millennia, Jerusalem has been the spiritual heart of Judaism. Even today, the city's demographic makeup reflects its Jewish heritage, with Jews constituting a clear majority since at least the Ottoman era. How is it possible that the capital of a sovereign Jewish state, with such deep ties to Jewish history and religion, is treated as a matter of international dispute?

This reluctance also reveals a broader double standard. Western nations routinely respect the capitals designated by other nations, even when contested. For example, they recognize Ankara as the capital of Turkey, despite historic claims to Istanbul, and Islamabad as Pakistan's capital, despite its contested location in Kashmir. Yet when it comes to Israel, they insist on an unprecedented level of ambiguity, deferring to international bodies like the United Nations or pandering to Arab and Muslim sentiment.

This posture not only undermines Israel's sovereignty but also emboldens those who seek to delegitimize the Jewish connection to Jerusalem. By refusing to recognize the city as Israel's rightful capital, the Western world perpetuates a false narrative that Jerusalem's status is somehow negotiable. It's a narrative rooted not in historical accuracy or fairness but in political expediency and economic fear.

The Role of Economic Interests

So why do these nations, who champion self-determination and democracy, fail to acknowledge the obvious? A primary explanation seems to be fear of economic retaliation from the Arab and Muslim world, particularly in the form of oil embargoes or loss of trade. The 1973 oil crisis, triggered by OPEC's retaliation against nations perceived as supporting Israel, left a lasting scar on the West's collective memory. Many European countries are acutely aware of their dependency on Middle Eastern oil and the potential fallout of angering powerful Arab nations.

Beyond oil, Arab and Muslim-majority countries represent significant trade markets for Western nations. Recognizing Jerusalem could jeopardize these relationships, leading to boycotts, loss of lucrative contracts, and reduced access to vital resources. European countries, in particular, have strong economic ties with the Middle East and have traditionally taken a more cautious approach to avoid jeopardizing these relationships.

The question remains: How long will Western nations allow fear and pragmatism to dictate their policies at the expense of truth and justice? Recognizing Jerusalem as the capital of Israel is not just about supporting a close ally—it's about respecting history, sovereignty, and the undeniable Jewish connection to Jerusalem.

Looking Ahead

Jerusalem stands at the crossroads of faith, history, and power. For millennia it has inspired devotion and conflict alike — the holiest city for Jews, central to Christianity, and deeply revered in Islam. Yet behind centuries of competing claims lies a simple historical truth: **Jerusalem has always been at the heart of Jewish civilization.** Long before modern Zionism or the State of Israel, Jews were not outsiders but the city's largest and most enduring community, a fact recorded by travelers, diplomats, and official censuses throughout the Ottoman and British Mandate periods.

In the modern era, movements like Hamas have twisted Jerusalem's sacred symbols into instruments of incitement, exploiting faith to inflame hatred and deny Jewish history. Archaeology, scripture, and continuous Jewish presence all tell a different story — one of unbroken connection, survival, and return.

But as Jewish life in Jerusalem endured, a new chapter was about to unfold. Under British rule, Jewish communities faced both Arab violence and foreign restrictions that threatened their survival and freedom. Out of that struggle emerged underground defense organizations — the Haganah, Irgun, and Lehi — that would carry the ancient spirit of resistance into the modern fight for independence.

Chapter 5

The Jewish Resistance

The history of Jewish resistance in Palestine is one of passion, bravery, and heartbreak. For centuries, the Jewish people in their ancestral homeland endured foreign rule and oppression, all while dreaming of reclaiming their independence. Under Ottoman rule, they defended their communities against constant threats, laying the groundwork for organized resistance. During the British Mandate, this struggle evolved into a fierce and coordinated fight against occupation. Along the way, incredible stories of courage, sacrifice, and defiance emerged, shaping the destiny of a people determined to achieve freedom.

Ottoman Rule: Laying the Groundwork for Resistance

Under Ottoman rule, Jews lived under the empire's *millet* system, which treated them as second-class citizens. Attacks by local bandits and Arab groups were common, forcing Jews to organize self-defense units such as **Bar Giora** and later **Hashomer** ("The Watchman"), which defended Jewish farms and villages.

One of the most gripping stories of this time is that of **Sarah Aaronsohn**, born in 1890 in Zikhron Ya'akov, a Jewish town in Ottoman Palestine. At just 25, she founded the **NILI spy network**, an acronym for the Hebrew phrase *"Netzah Yisrael Lo Yeshaker"* ("The Glory of Israel Does Not Deceive"). The network provided intelligence to the British to help defeat the Ottomans during World War I. When Sarah was captured, she endured days of torture without revealing her comrades. In her final act of defiance, she took her own life to protect the network. To this day, she remains a symbol of Jewish courage and devotion.

During World War I, many Jews volunteered to serve in the **Zion Mule Corps**, a military unit established in 1915 and led by **Joseph**

Trumpeldor, a one-armed war hero whose motto *"It is good to die for our country"* later inspired generations. The Zion Mule Corps fought valiantly in the **Gallipoli Campaign**, marking the first time in centuries that Jews had formed a recognized military unit under their own flag.

As the war continued, another unit—the **Jewish Legion**—was created in 1917. Among its members was **David Ben-Gurion**, the future prime minister of Israel. The Legion fought alongside the British Army in the campaign to liberate Palestine from Ottoman rule, and its participation in the liberation of Jerusalem was profoundly symbolic. After two thousand years of exile and foreign domination, Jewish soldiers once again marched into their eternal city under a flag of their own.

David Ben-Gurion, who would later become Israel's first Prime Minister, serving as a private in the Jewish Legion during World War I. Formed in 1917, the Legion fought alongside the British Army against the Ottoman Empire.
Source: Wikimedia Commons / Public Domain

The Jewish Legion, formally composed of several battalions under the British Army's Royal Fusiliers, played an active role in key campaigns of the Middle Eastern theater during World War I. Units such as the 38th, 39th, and 40th Battalions of the Royal Fusiliers fought under the command of General Edmund Allenby in operations stretching from Egypt and Sinai to the Jordan Valley and the Judean Hills. Their most notable engagement came in 1918 at the Battle of Megiddo, a decisive Allied victory that broke Ottoman resistance in Palestine. Jewish Legion troops also participated in securing the Jordan River crossings and took part in guarding supply routes leading into Jerusalem.

An armband for the Jewish Legion from 1917, with that era's Zionist motif - a Star of David with the word "Zion" ('Tziyon') in Hebrew located in the center.
Source: Public Domain

The British Mandate: Hope Turns to Resistance

When the British took control of Palestine in 1920 under the Mandate system, Jews initially welcomed them. After all, the **Balfour Declaration** of 1917 had promised to support the establishment of a Jewish homeland. But this hope soon turned into disillusionment.

British policies began to shift as they sought to appease Arab leaders across the Middle East. Restrictions on Jewish immigration and land purchases became harsher, and British authorities used administrative power to halt the Zionist project's momentum. The situation became dire when the Nazis rose to power in Germany. Millions of Jews across Europe sought refuge, yet the gates of Palestine remained largely closed.

The most infamous of these restrictions came with the **1939 White Paper**, which limited Jewish immigration to only 75,000 people over five years—just **15,000 per year**—at the exact moment when millions were being hunted down in Europe's ghettos and concentration camps. It was a moral catastrophe disguised as policy. The same Britain that had promised a "national home for the Jewish people" now condemned them to die by denying them one.

British forces imposed naval blockades, intercepting ships carrying Holocaust survivors and sending them back to Europe. Refugees who managed to reach the shores of Palestine were detained in camps such as Atlit near Haifa, fenced in behind barbed wire as if they were prisoners rather than survivors.

The Tragedy of the Refugee Ships

Perhaps no symbol captures British cruelty more vividly than the refugee ships. These vessels carried the final hopes of Europe's surviving Jews — men, women, and children who had escaped the Nazi inferno only to find the gates of their ancestral homeland locked by the very empire that claimed to defend "civilization" and "human rights."

The most famous case was the **Exodus 1947**, carrying more than 4,500 Holocaust survivors from displaced-persons camps in France. When the ship neared the shores of Palestine, British destroyers rammed and boarded it violently, killing three passengers and wounding dozens. The British then forced the survivors onto prison ships and sent them — unbelievably — back to Germany.

The world watched in disbelief as photographs showed Jewish survivors being marched off ships under British rifles in Hamburg, the same country that had built the gas chambers. That single event shattered whatever moral legitimacy the British Mandate still had. The image of those refugees—stateless, beaten, and humiliated once again—did more to turn global opinion toward the Zionist cause than any speech or petition ever could.

The tragedy of the **Struma** stands as another chilling indictment. In 1942, this decrepit Romanian ship, carrying 769 Jewish refugees, tried to reach Palestine after being denied entry to Turkey. The British refused to allow the passengers to disembark and ordered the vessel to be towed back into the open Black Sea without food, water, or a functioning engine. Days later, the ship exploded and sank, killing everyone on board except one person. The cause of the explosion remains disputed—some blame a Soviet submarine—but the moral responsibility was unmistakable: Britain's policy of exclusion had condemned nearly eight hundred souls to death at sea.

The **Patria** tragedy in 1940 added yet another dark chapter. Packed with Jewish refugees from Central Europe, the ship was detained by the British in Haifa harbor. Desperate to prevent deportation, members of the Haganah planted a small explosive meant to disable the vessel. The explosion was far stronger than intended, and the ship sank, killing over 260 Jews. Though the Haganah bore the immediate blame, the root cause was again the British blockade — a policy so merciless that it drove desperate Jews to sabotage their own ships rather than be sent back to Nazi-occupied Europe.

Nor were these isolated incidents. The **Mefküre**, **Henrietta Szold**, and **Tiger Hill** were among many other refugee ships intercepted, turned away, or sunk under tragic circumstances. The Mediterranean became a graveyard for Jews fleeing genocide. Between 1939 and 1945, more than 1,500 Jewish refugees drowned because of British restrictions on immigration to Palestine.

These were not the acts of a colonial power maintaining order. They were the acts of a government choosing political expediency over human life

— fearing Arab anger more than Jewish annihilation. While Jewish refugees were dying at sea, British officials in London were writing memoranda about "maintaining stability" and "preserving balance." It was a bureaucratic cruelty wrapped in polite language, carried out with chilling precision.

The Resistance Fighters: Heroes of Defiance

As British repression intensified, the Jewish underground movements grew bolder, more organized, and more determined. Three main groups came to define this struggle: **the Haganah**, **the Irgun (Etzel)**, and **Lehi (the Stern Gang)**. Though their methods differed, their purpose was identical — to liberate their homeland from foreign rule and secure a future for the Jewish people.

The **Haganah**, originally formed to defend Jewish farms and settlements, evolved into a vast underground army. Its intelligence network penetrated British institutions, its supply chains smuggled weapons under the noses of British patrols, and its secret immigration network — Aliyah Bet — became a lifeline for tens of thousands of Holocaust survivors. Under the cover of night, rickety ships packed with refugees approached the shores of Palestine. Many were intercepted, but others slipped through, greeted by Haganah units who helped the survivors disappear into sympathetic communities. Every successful landing was not only a rescue — it was an act of defiance against the British blockade.

While the Haganah operated more cautiously, the **Irgun**, led by **Menachem Begin**, and **Lehi**, founded by **Avraham Stern**, took a far more militant approach. They targeted railways, police stations, British military convoys, and administrative buildings — not out of hatred, but out of desperation. Every attack was meant to send a message: "We will no longer be ruled by foreigners in our own land."

A Haganah ship carrying Holocaust refugees from Europe
Source: Wikimedia Commons / Public Domain.

One of the most daring operations of this period was the King David Hotel bombing in 1946, carried out by the Irgun. The hotel served as the British administrative and military headquarters in Jerusalem — the nerve center of Mandate control. Irgun fighters disguised as Arab laborers planted explosives in the basement and sent repeated warnings to evacuate the building. The British ignored the warnings, and the explosion killed 91 people. It remains controversial to this day, but its message was unmistakable: Jewish resistance would not be silenced, and the cost of occupation would no longer be borne only by the Jews.

The British called them "terrorists" but history calls them freedom fighters. Menachem Begin, once hunted by the British as a criminal, would one day sit in the prime minister's chair of the State of Israel. His comrades — men like Yitzhak Shamir, Moshe Sneh, and Avraham Stern — would become ministers, diplomats, and founders of a nation that rose from the ashes of exile and oppression.

A female Haganah officer demonstrating the handling of a Sten gun.
Source: Hagana Museum / Wikimedia Commons / Public Domain.

One forgotten detail from this period is the true origin of the phrase **"Free Palestine."** Today, the slogan is shouted by those who seek Israel's destruction, but in the 1940s, it meant something entirely different. The phrase was born from the Zionist struggle for Jewish independence. The **Irgun** worked closely with an American organization called the **American League for a Free Palestine (ALFP),** led by figures such as Hillel Kook. The ALFP ran newspaper ads, held rallies, and broadcast radio programs across the United States, demanding freedom for the Jewish homeland from British occupation. Their posters showed barbed wire around the map of Palestine with the words "Free Palestine — Let My People Go." The movement even lobbied Congress and met with senators to demand an end to the British Mandate.

For them, "Free Palestine" meant exactly what it said — free it for the Jewish people, whose homeland was being held hostage by imperial power.

The phrase has since been hijacked and twisted into a slogan for Israel's erasure — an irony lost on most who chant it today. The same words that once symbolized Jewish liberation are now wielded as a weapon against the very state those fighters helped create.

For the Jewish resistance of the 1940s, freedom was not an abstract dream. It was paid for in blood, carried on forged papers, hidden in smuggled arms, and whispered through prison walls. These were not colonizers seeking conquest; they were survivors demanding dignity — men and women who rose from the ruins of Europe to reclaim the only home they had ever truly known.

British Atrocities and Double Standards

As Jewish resistance intensified, British tactics grew increasingly brutal. Collective punishment became standard policy: entire towns and neighborhoods were placed under curfew, homes were demolished, and mass arrests filled the detention camps in Atlit, Rafah, and Latrun. British soldiers patrolled Jewish streets at night, dragging men from their homes for interrogations, often beating them in front of their families.

Captured resistance fighters were subjected to torture and public executions in British prisons such as Acre, Jerusalem Central Prison, and the citadel in Jaffa. The gallows became the British Empire's final argument against Jewish independence. Fighters from the Irgun and Lehi were hanged publicly, their bodies displayed as warnings. Even the dead were humiliated — their families forbidden to mourn or attend burials.

The British oppression infuriated Jewish leaders. They were not colonizers but a people fighting to return home after 2,000 years of exile, yet they were treated as criminals in their own land. The British invoked the language of "law and order" to justify their actions while turning a blind eye to the violence of Arab militias that attacked Jewish settlements with impunity.

After every Arab riot, the pattern repeated: Jews were disarmed "to prevent escalation," while Arab mobs were rarely punished. British police and military units even coordinated with Arab gangs, sharing intelligence and overlooking massacres in Hebron (1929), Jaffa (1921), and Tiberias (1938).

British reports frequently described Arab attackers as "spontaneous rioters" but labeled Jewish defenders as "terrorists." The hypocrisy was staggering. When Jews built defensive walls around kibbutzim, they were accused of provocation; when they armed themselves, they were accused of militarism. But when they were slaughtered unarmed, the British offered sympathy — and no protection.

Jewish underground groups understood this duplicity. To them, the British were no longer the protectors of civilization but obstacles to survival. Men like Menachem Begin and Yitzhak Shamir came to see British policy not as misguided but as morally bankrupt. They realized that the same empire that preached freedom at the United Nations was still suppressing it with bayonets in Palestine.

By 1946, British forces had conducted more than **17,000 raids** on Jewish homes, arrested thousands without trial, and censored all Zionist publications. They declared martial law in Tel Aviv, bombed the headquarters of the Jewish Agency, and confiscated weapons meant to defend settlements from Arab attacks. The British even imprisoned Holocaust survivors who reached Palestine illegally — locking them in barbed-wire camps in Cyprus, a bitter echo of the concentration camps they had just escaped.

In the end, the British crackdown achieved the opposite of what it intended. Every hanging, every demolished home, every deported refugee deepened Jewish resolve. Resistance groups that once operated independently began to coordinate under a unified command, determined to drive the British out once and for all.

The British Empire wanted obedience. What it got instead was defiance — from a people who had learned through centuries of persecution that freedom is never given, only fought for.

Executions and Final Acts of Defiance

By 1947, the British campaign to crush Jewish resistance had reached its darkest and most ruthless phase. Dozens of captured fighters from the Irgun, Lehi, and Haganah filled British prisons across the land — Acre, Jerusalem, Latrun, and Jaffa. Many were sentenced to death by hanging. These young men, often barely in their twenties, faced execution not as criminals but as soldiers in a war for liberation.

The British intended these hangings to break Jewish morale. Instead, they became rallying cries for freedom. Each condemned fighter wrote farewell letters smuggled from prison, declaring unwavering loyalty to the dream of a Jewish homeland. In the streets, crowds gathered outside prison walls to sing "Hatikvah" — "The Hope" — as the gallows creaked behind the stone walls. Mothers wept, but the Yishuv stood prouder than ever. The British could hang bodies, but they could not hang a nation's spirit.

Among those sentenced to die were **Meir Feinstein** of the Irgun and **Moshe Barazani** of Lehi. Feinstein, a young man from Jerusalem, had lost his arm in battle and was captured after an attack on the Jerusalem railway station. Barazani, a Kurdish Jew from Iraq, had been caught carrying a grenade intended for a British officer. Both were sentenced to death in Jerusalem Central Prison — the same place where British flags flew above the gallows that had already claimed so many Jewish lives.

95

But Feinstein and Barazani refused to let the British claim theirs. On the eve of their execution, they hid a grenade inside an orange — smuggled in by their comrades disguised as prison visitors. As they sat together in their cell, they prayed, wrapped themselves in a flag, and embraced. Just before midnight, as the British guards prepared to lead them to the gallows, the explosion echoed through the prison. They had chosen to die as free men, not as prisoners of an empire that denied them dignity.

Their deaths stunned even their British jailers. The next morning, the guards entered to find the walls splattered with smoke and fragments of the flag. The official report described it coldly as a "suicide by explosion." But for the Jewish people, it was an act of sanctified defiance — a final victory over subjugation.

Menachem Begin, then leader of the Irgun, later said:

> *"The British could take their lives, but not their freedom. They died with their heads held high — martyrs of Israel's resurrection."*

Their story spread like wildfire across the Yishuv. Schoolchildren memorized their last letters. Underground newspapers printed their portraits beside the words **"They lit the path to freedom."** Their cell in Jerusalem's Russian Compound became a place of pilgrimage after independence, preserved exactly as it was that night — two iron beds, a small table, and a wall still bearing the marks of the explosion.

Feinstein and Barazani were not alone. Many others — like **Dov Gruner**, **Eliezer Kashani**, and **Yaakov Weiss** — went to the gallows singing Hebrew songs and saluting the Jewish flag. Some kissed the rope that was meant to hang them. Their courage shocked even their British executioners, who were accustomed to silence and fear. The executioner, an Englishman named Thomas Pierpoint, later confessed he had "never seen men die like this — calm, smiling, without a tremor."

These were not terrorists or fanatics. They were freedom fighters, patriots of a people who had waited 2,000 years to be free again. Their deaths became immortal symbols of sacrifice — the final notes of a struggle that would soon culminate in victory.

Only one year later, the British flag that flew over their prison came down for good. The gallows they once used to hang Jewish fighters now stood in a land reborn — the **State of Israel** — built on the courage, pain, and devotion of those who refused to bow.

Liberation and Legacy

By the late 1940s, the British Mandate was collapsing under the weight of relentless Jewish resistance, international outrage, and global sympathy for the survivors of the Holocaust. Britain's empire, once proud and sprawling, was crumbling in every direction — from India to Kenya to Palestine. Weary, demoralized, and shamed by its own hypocrisy, Britain announced in 1947 that it would withdraw from Palestine and turn the issue over to the newly formed United Nations.

That same year, the UN voted to partition the land into Jewish and Arab states. For the Jews, it was the long-awaited acknowledgment of what they had fought and died for. For the Arabs, it was a call to arms. The British prepared to leave, and the Jewish underground prepared for the war that everyone knew was coming.

The **Haganah**, once an underground defense force, transformed into a national army — the **Israel Defense Forces (IDF)**. Fighters from the **Irgun** and **Lehi**, once branded as outlaws, were absorbed into its ranks. They set aside their internal rivalries and united under one flag, one purpose: to defend the newborn Jewish state against annihilation.

When David Ben-Gurion proclaimed Israel's independence on **May 14, 1948**, it was not a gift of the international community. It was the hard-earned triumph of a people who had fought for every inch of legitimacy, every life saved, every refugee landed, and every bullet smuggled under

British watch. The Declaration of Independence was signed in Tel Aviv under the shadow of Arab armies already advancing from all directions.

What began as underground resistance had become the organized defense of a reborn nation. Those once hunted by the British as "terrorists" now became the founders and protectors of the State of Israel. The same hands that had built clandestine printing presses, laid bombs under rail lines, and forged false identity papers now built hospitals, universities, and cities.

The young men and women of the resistance — Feinstein, Barazani, Begin, Shamir, and countless others — passed from the shadows of occupation into the light of sovereignty. Their names filled the first ranks of the Israeli army, parliament, and cabinet. The nation they fought to resurrect now stood tall, free, and unbowed — a testament to their courage.

The British left in silence. The gallows they once used to hang Jewish fighters stood empty. The Union Jack was lowered, and in its place rose the blue and white flag of Israel — the Star of David gleaming under the sun of independence.

Prelude to War: Arab Violence Before 1948

As Britain prepared to withdraw, Arab hostility toward the Jewish community was already boiling over. Palestinian Arabs were not passive bystanders waiting for the political outcome of partition — they had been waging war against the Jewish population long before 1948. The so-called "civil war" that erupted after the UN partition vote in November 1947 was, in truth, the continuation of a campaign that had begun decades earlier.

Armed Arab militias, including the *Arab Liberation Army* and the *Army of the Holy War*, launched coordinated attacks on Jewish towns, villages, and supply routes. Jerusalem itself came under siege, with Arab forces cutting off the main highway from Tel Aviv and starving the city's Jewish population of food, medicine, and ammunition. Jewish convoys attempting to reach the city were ambushed and massacred — most infamously the Hadassah medical convoy, in which doctors, nurses, and patients were slaughtered on their way to Mount Scopus.

But the roots of this violence stretched far deeper. The slogan *"Itbah al-Yahud"* — "Slaughter the Jews" — echoed through riots and pogroms long before the State of Israel existed. Jewish communities in the Land of Israel had endured centuries of persecution under foreign rule. The 1517 massacres during Ottoman conquest, the 1834 Safed pogrom, and the 1920 Nebi Musa riots all left deep scars. The 1929 Hebron massacre — in which Arab mobs butchered 67 Jews and destroyed one of Judaism's oldest communities — and the 1936–1939 Arab Revolt further revealed that this was no anti-colonial struggle, but a sustained campaign to eliminate Jewish presence from the land entirely.

By the time the British left Palestine, the conflict was already in full swing. The Jewish community — outnumbered, under siege, and abandoned by the Mandate authorities — was forced to fight not only for independence, but for survival.

Chapter 6

The Establishment of Israel

The Partition and the Rejection

On November 29, 1947, the United Nations voted on **Resolution 181**, which proposed partitioning British-ruled Palestine into two states — one Jewish and one Arab. The Jewish state would cover only a small fraction of the land promised in the Balfour Declaration — disconnected, narrow, and demographically uncertain — yet the Jewish leadership accepted it. After 2,000 years of exile and persecution, even a sliver of sovereignty in their ancestral homeland was worth embracing.

What most people don't realize is that the original British Mandate for Palestine, established in 1920, included all of what is now Jordan. But Britain unilaterally split the Mandate in two and handed roughly 78% of the land east of the Jordan River to the Arabs, creating Transjordan, which became the country Jordan in 1946. That left less than 22% of the original Mandate for the Jewish homeland west of the Jordan River.

When the UN proposed partitioning that remaining sliver in 1947, the Jews were offered only about 55% of it — and even that was misleading. Nearly 60% of the Jewish portion was the barren Negev Desert, sparsely populated and lacking water. In practical terms, the Jewish state would have controlled only about 12% of the original territory of Mandatory Palestine. And yet, they accepted it — grateful for any chance, however small, to restore Jewish sovereignty in their ancestral homeland.

The Arab response was immediate and violent. Not a single Arab delegation accepted the plan. The Arab League declared flatly that it would oppose partition "by force of arms." Even before the British withdrew, Arab militias began attacking Jewish neighborhoods, buses, and villages. The so-called "civil war" phase of the 1947–48 conflict had begun — the opening act of Israel's war for survival.

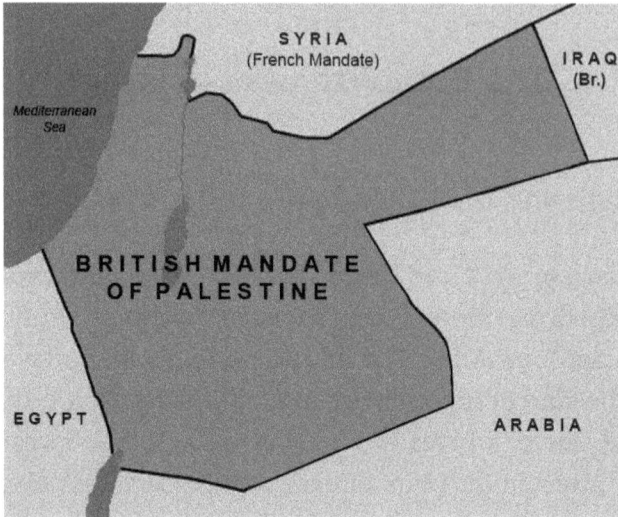

*Map of the original **British Mandate for Palestine (1920)**, which included all the territory both west and east of the Jordan River. In 1922, Britain carved off roughly **78% of the land** to create **Transjordan** (modern-day Jordan), leaving less than **22%** of the original Mandate for the prospective Jewish homeland.*

The Civil War in Palestine (1947–1948)

Within hours of the UN vote, coordinated attacks broke out across the country. Arab irregulars and local militias — aided by volunteers from Syria and Iraq — launched a campaign to destroy the Yishuv, the Jewish community in Palestine. They cut off roads, sabotaged supply routes, and besieged Jewish neighborhoods.

The fiercest battle raged around Jerusalem. Nearly 100,000 Jews were trapped inside the city, surrounded by Arab villages controlling the hills that overlooked the only road from Tel Aviv. Food, medicine, and water ran dangerously low. Arab fighters led by Abd al-Qadir al-Husseini ambushed every convoy, turning the lifeline to Jerusalem into a death trap.

One of the darkest days came on April 13, 1948, when a medical convoy to the **Hadassah Hospital on Mount Scopus** was attacked. Seventy-eight doctors, nurses, and patients were massacred. British troops stationed nearby did nothing. Burned ambulances and charred bodies became the symbol of both Arab cruelty and British indifference.

Desperate to save the city, the Haganah launched **Operation Nachshon**, the first large-scale Jewish offensive, to open the supply road. Young volunteers fought their way through entrenched Arab positions, many dying in the attempt. Though many convoys were lost, the temporary success of Nachshon broke the siege and showed that coordinated Jewish forces could go on the offensive — a critical psychological turning point.

The Grand Mufti's Nazi Alliance

No figure better embodied the ideological hatred fueling Arab opposition to Jews than the Grand Mufti of Jerusalem, Haj Amin al-Husseini. Appointed by the British in the 1920s, the Mufti used his religious authority to incite violent uprisings against Jews, turning mosques and radio broadcasts into tools of propaganda. But his influence reached far beyond Palestine.

In 1941, al-Husseini fled to Berlin and met with Adolf Hitler, Heinrich Himmler, and other senior Nazi officials. The Mufti pledged his full support for the Axis cause and discussed plans to extend the "Final Solution" to the Jews of Palestine and the Middle East once Rommel's army reached Egypt. He broadcast antisemitic propaganda over Nazi radio, recruited tens of thousands of Muslims into the Waffen-SS, and urged them to "kill the Jews wherever you find them."

These recruits formed units that participated in mass killings in Yugoslavia and Eastern Europe — directly contributing to the Holocaust. After the war, al-Husseini escaped prosecution and returned to the Arab world as a hero, continuing to preach the same genocidal ideology that had driven his alliance with Hitler.

The Grand Mufti of Jerusalem meeting with Adolf Hitler, Berlin, November 28, 1941.
Source: Bundesarchiv, Bild 146-1987-004-09A / Heinrich Hoffmann / CC-BY-SA 3.0.

This was the moral and ideological foundation upon which much of the Arab world approached 1948: a war not over borders, but over existence itself.

The British Departure and the Arab Invasion

By early 1948, Britain's empire was crumbling. Its soldiers wanted out of Palestine, not to die for a mandate no one wanted. In their retreat, they left chaos behind. British officers confiscated Jewish weapons but left Arab arsenals untouched. They patrolled Jewish neighborhoods while ignoring Arab gunmen. Entire Jewish towns were disarmed, while the British high command quietly coordinated with Arab leaders to ensure a "smooth transition."

On **May 14, 1948**, as the last British High Commissioner sailed from Haifa, **David Ben-Gurion** declared independence in Tel Aviv:

> *"The Land of Israel was the birthplace of the Jewish people... Here they first attained statehood... Here they created cultural values of national and universal significance."*

Within twenty-four hours, Israel was invaded. Five Arab armies —
Egypt, Jordan, Syria, Lebanon, and Iraq — launched a full-scale
assault. The goal was not borders, not compromise — annihilation. Arab
League Secretary-General **Azzam Pasha** vowed a "war of extermination
and a momentous massacre."

A War Against All Odds

At independence, Israel had about **35,000 fighters** — many untrained
and half unarmed. It had **no tanks, no artillery, and no air force.**
Makeshift "armored cars" were buses welded with scrap metal,
sarcastically called *"sandwich cars."*

*A bullet-riddled **Jewish supply convoy vehicle** destroyed during the **Siege of
Jerusalem (1948)**. With no tanks or armored vehicles, Jewish forces improvised by
bolting steel plates onto buses and trucks to protect convoys bringing food, medicine,
and ammunition to the besieged city.*
Source: Wikimedia Commons / Public Domain

In contrast, the invading Arab armies were among the most heavily armed in the region:

- **Jordan's Arab Legion**, led by **British General John Glubb ("Glubb Pasha")**, was Britain's pride in the Middle East — disciplined, modern, and fully armed with **British tanks, artillery, and armored vehicles**.

- **Egypt** invaded from the south with **Spitfire warplanes, C-47 bombers**, and **British-supplied tanks**, joined by thousands of **Muslim Brotherhood** volunteers.

- **Iraq** sent mechanized divisions trained by British officers, backed by intelligence from the **Royal Air Force**.

- **Syria** and **Lebanon**, both armed and trained by **France**, attacked from the north with French tanks and field guns.

- Several **Nazi officers** who had escaped postwar justice found refuge in Arab capitals and joined the fight, applying the same murderous ideology in a new war against the Jews.

The imbalance was staggering. The Arab coalition began with **60,000 troops, over 200 tanks, hundreds of artillery guns, more than 120 warplanes and dozens of bombers**. By the war's end, the number swelled to over 100,000 soldiers.

	Arab Armies	Israel (1948)
Troops	~60,000+ (100,000+ later)	~35,000 militia
Tanks & Armored Vehicles	200+	0
Artillery	Hundreds	0 (later smuggled some)
Warplanes	120+	0 (few Czech planes later)
Bombers/Transport	Dozens	0

Israel's fighters — many fresh from concentration camps — faced them with smuggled Czech rifles and homemade explosives. When the United

States and Britain imposed an **arms embargo** on the region, it only crippled Israel; the Arab states kept receiving British and French arms without restriction.

Israel's first military workshops built mortars out of plumbing pipes and armor from steel doors. Every bullet mattered. Every rifle was shared. And every loss carried the weight of survival.

So Israel wasn't just fighting five Arab states — it was fighting British and French proxy armies. The Jordanian Arab Legion was commanded by **British General John Glubb** and staffed with other British officers like **Brigadier Norman Lash**, who led the assault on Jerusalem that ended with the expulsion of its Jewish residents. The Egyptian army used British tanks, artillery, and Spitfires, while Syria and Lebanon fielded French-trained forces with French weapons.

King Abdullah I of Transjordan (left) with British General John Bagot Glubb ("Glubb Pasha"), commander of the British-trained Arab Legion. Under Glubb's command, the Arab Legion invaded Israel in 1948, seized East Jerusalem, and expelled its ancient Jewish population — all while operating with full British funding, arms, and oversight. Source: Wikimedia Commons (public domain)

The Battle for Jerusalem

No battle was more desperate than Jerusalem. After the British withdrawal, the **Arab Legion** under British Brigadier Norman Lash surrounded the city and began shelling Jewish neighborhoods daily. The Old City's Jewish Quarter, home to families whose ancestors had lived there for centuries, was besieged and starved into surrender.

On May 28, 1948, it fell. The remaining 1,500 Jews were expelled — the first ethnic cleansing of Jerusalem in modern history. The Hurva Synagogue, centuries old, was blown up. Jewish homes were looted and burned. Gravestones from the Mount of Olives cemetery were ripped out and used to pave roads and latrines for Jordanian and British soldiers. The Western Wall, Judaism's holiest accessible site, was sealed off for the next nineteen years.

Yet even as East Jerusalem fell, West Jerusalem survived. In one of the war's most astonishing feats, Jewish volunteers carved a new supply route through the Judean hills — the Burma Road — under constant enemy fire. Trucks crawled along the steep dirt track, bringing food and ammunition into the starving city. Against all odds, Jerusalem lived.

Turning the Tide

Despite overwhelming odds, Israel adapted with breathtaking speed. The Haganah became a national army — the **Israel Defense Forces (IDF)** — unifying the Irgun, Lehi, and Palmach under a single command. Czechoslovakia, defying the global embargo, sent Israel its first lifeline: rifles, machine guns, and Messerschmitt planes. Within months, the Jews who began the war with nothing now had the means to fight back.

Key campaigns turned the tide:

- **Operation Nachshon** (April 1948): opened the road to Jerusalem.

- **Operation Yiftach** (May 1948): liberated the Galilee.

- **Operation Danny** (July 1948): captured Lod and Ramle, securing the Tel Aviv–Jerusalem corridor.

- **Operation Yoav** (October 1948): shattered Egyptian lines in the Negev.

- **Operation Horev** (December 1948): drove the Egyptian army completely out of Israeli territory.

Every victory came at immense cost — over 6,000 Israelis, nearly 1 percent of the Jewish population, were killed. But by early 1949, the unthinkable had happened: the young Jewish state had survived.

Jerusalem Reborn, but Divided

The 1949 Armistice left Jerusalem physically and politically divided. The eastern part of the city, including the Old City and the Temple Mount, came under Jordanian control, and Jews were completely denied access to their holiest sites. The western half became part of Israel and gradually developed into the country's functioning capital, even though most of the international community did not formally recognize it. Life in Jewish Jerusalem was marked by both rebuilding and resilience — neighborhoods had been destroyed, families displaced, and access to sacred places cut off, yet the city continued to grow. The old phrase "Next Year in Jerusalem," once a line from prayer, took on a new, practical meaning — a quiet but enduring commitment that the city would one day be whole again.

The Nakba: A Tragic Consequence, Not a Crime

The Arab world calls it *al-Nakba* — "the catastrophe." In their narrative, it marks the mass displacement of Palestinians in 1948, a tragedy often described as deliberate ethnic cleansing. But the historical record tells a far more complex story. The Nakba was not a pre-planned Israeli campaign to expel Arabs. It was the direct consequence of a war launched by five invading Arab armies and the chaos that followed.

When Israel declared independence on May 14, 1948, its population was still reeling from the Holocaust. Twenty-four hours later, Egypt, Jordan, Syria, Lebanon, and Iraq invaded the newborn state. Their declared goal was not a border dispute or political protest — it was extermination. Arab leaders and radio broadcasts openly called for a *"momentous massacre"* of the Jews. Against this backdrop, the flight of many Arab civilians was not the result of premeditated Israeli policy, but the natural outcome of a brutal regional war.

Many Arabs fled simply out of fear — fear of bombings, advancing armies, or rumors of massacres spread by both sides. Others were urged to evacuate by their own leaders, who promised they would return once the Jewish state had been destroyed. Former Syrian Prime Minister **Khalid al-Azm** later admitted in his memoirs:

> *"We brought destruction upon the refugees, urging them to leave their homes temporarily so that the Arab armies could crush the Zionists and drive them into the sea."*

Some Arab residents were indeed expelled during combat operations, particularly in strategic areas or villages used by enemy fighters. But these were wartime measures taken under existential threat, not a systematic campaign of expulsion.

The irony often overlooked is that the Nakba, tragic as it was, may have saved the Jewish state from annihilation. When the Arab armies invaded, Israel faced an impossible situation — just 35,000 fighters, many without rifles, no tanks, and no air force, against more than 60,000 troops equipped with British and French armor, artillery, and warplanes. Had large Arab populations remained inside Israel's borders, many of whom were openly sympathetic to the invading forces, Israel's chances of survival would have been far lower.

The sudden depopulation of hostile areas allowed Israel to focus its limited manpower on the front lines rather than internal defense. Supply routes, especially to besieged Jerusalem, became easier to secure. Morale within Jewish ranks solidified around a clear understanding: the war was not about land or politics, but about survival.

While the displacement of civilians is always tragic, history must be honest about cause and effect. The Nakba was born from a war that the Arab world chose — a war declared against a one-day-old state still burying the ashes of European Jewry. Israel's victory, and the resulting refugee crisis, were two sides of the same event. One marked the rebirth of a nation; the other, the self-inflicted wound of leaders who gambled on genocide and lost.

The Forgotten Jewish Refugees

The story of 1948 is not complete without its missing half — the one the world rarely mentions. While Arab leaders lament the *Nakba*, nearly **850,000 Jews** across the Middle East and North Africa were simultaneously expelled or forced to flee their homes. From Baghdad to Cairo, Damascus to Tripoli, entire Jewish communities — some dating back more than 2,500 years — were wiped out in a few short years.

After Israel's independence, Arab regimes unleashed waves of persecution against their Jewish citizens. Synagogues were torched, businesses looted, and Jewish-owned properties seized by the state. In Iraq, Jews were publicly hanged. In Egypt, they were stripped of citizenship. In Yemen and Libya, they fled under gunfire. What began as intimidation soon became state policy: Jews were no longer welcome anywhere in the Arab world.

Most of these refugees found only one safe haven — Israel. They arrived with nothing but the clothes on their backs, often airlifted by Israel in daring rescue operations like *Operation Magic Carpet* (1949–1950), which brought more than 49,000 Yemenite Jews to safety, and

Operation Ezra and Nehemiah (1950–1952), which rescued over 120,000 Jews from Iraq. Within a few years, these destitute refugees became integral to Israel's rebirth — building towns, farming the Negev, serving in the army, and helping forge a unified national identity.

Meanwhile, the Arab world chose a different path. Rather than integrating Palestinian refugees, Arab governments confined them to camps and stripped them of basic rights. In countries like Lebanon, Syria, and Jordan, generations of Palestinians were deliberately kept stateless — not out of compassion, but as a political weapon. Their suffering became a propaganda tool to perpetuate hostility against Israel.

Both populations suffered uprooting and loss. But only one side turned tragedy into nation-building. The Jewish refugees of the Arab world did not remain victims. They became citizens, soldiers, and builders — proof that resilience, not grievance, is what creates a nation.

While nearly a million Jews were being expelled from Arab countries, something remarkable was unfolding inside Israel itself. In stark contrast to the treatment of Jews in Arab lands, Israel chose a different path. Despite the devastation of war and the chaos of independence, the new Jewish state granted full citizenship and equal rights to the Arab population that remained within its borders. The same year that ancient Jewish communities across the Middle East were being erased, a new Arab minority was being integrated into Israel's democracy — protected by law, represented in parliament, and free to live, work, and worship as they chose.

Israeli Arabs: A Minority That Stayed

Despite the chaos of war, not all Arabs fled in 1948. Around **156,000 Arabs** remained within the borders of the newly established State of Israel, primarily in Galilee, Haifa, Jaffa, and the Negev. Contrary to the widespread myth of mass expulsion, these Arabs were **not driven out—** they stayed, rebuilt, and became citizens of the new Jewish state. In a region where defeated populations were often massacred or displaced, their survival and enfranchisement were exceptional.

From its first days, Israel made a deliberate choice that defied regional norms: rather than exact revenge or impose subjugation, it extended full citizenship and equal legal rights to those Arabs who remained. They were granted the right to vote, to run for office, to serve in the courts, and to participate in every aspect of civic life. This decision was not merely pragmatic—it reflected Israel's foundational ethos as a democratic state rooted in Jewish values of justice and human dignity.

Over the decades, this minority has grown to over **two million citizens**, roughly 21% of Israel's population. Today, Israeli Arabs—Muslims, Christians, Druze, and Bedouins—are represented at every level of public life. They sit in the Knesset, serve as Supreme Court justices, lead major hospitals and universities, and even command units within the Israel Defense Forces, particularly among Druze and Bedouin communities. In recent years, Arab parties have even held the balance of power in Israeli coalition governments—something unimaginable in most of the Arab world.

This reality stands in stark contrast to the fate of Jews in Arab countries. While ancient Jewish communities across Iraq, Egypt, Yemen, and Syria were wiped out through expulsions, confiscations, and violence, Israel integrated its Arab population into a shared civic framework. The same years that saw Jews stripped of citizenship and livelihoods in the Arab world also saw Arabs in Israel voting, studying in universities, and gaining access to healthcare and education under the Jewish state.

The story of Israeli Arabs exposes a profound moral irony: while the Arab world erased its Jewish minorities, Israel—surrounded by enemies—protected and empowered its Arab citizens. In a Middle East dominated by autocracies and sectarian divisions, Israel remains the only country where Arabs and Jews share equal democratic rights under the law, side by side in courts, hospitals, universities, and city halls.

The Birth of Israel

By the war's end in 1949, Israel had not only survived — it had expanded beyond the UN partition borders. The armistice agreements granted Israel control of about 78 percent of the former Mandate territory, while Jordan annexed the West Bank and Egypt occupied Gaza.

Israel's victory wasn't a miracle of luck — it was a triumph of determination. Every soldier knew that defeat meant extermination. For a people who had walked through Auschwitz only three years earlier, surrender was unthinkable.

The establishment of Israel was not a Western colonial project — it was a Jewish revolution. A people without a country, without tanks, without allies, reclaimed their homeland through unity, ingenuity, and sheer will.

From Destruction to Redemption

Israel's victory in 1948 was not only military — it was moral. A people once scattered, stateless, and hunted reclaimed their destiny. They turned buses into armored cars, and forged weapons in secret workshops. Refugees became soldiers; survivors became founders.

In months, despair turned into determination and exile into independence. The Jewish people restored their ancient language, revived their homeland, and raised a flag unseen for two thousand years. The same people once herded into ghettos now stood guard over their own borders — free and sovereign.

Israel's rebirth was not a gift but a triumph of will. Against impossible odds, the Jewish people proved that survival is not endurance but strength. After millennia of exile, they had returned — not as victims of history, but as its authors.

Chapter 7
The Invention of a Palestinian National Identity (1964)

The so-called *Palestinian national identity* is a modern political construct—engineered, not inherited. Unlike nations that arise from shared language, culture, or historic continuity, the Palestinian identity was assembled in the mid-20th century as a tool of political warfare against Israel. It was not born from an organic peoplehood but manufactured by Arab regimes to deny Jewish sovereignty and sustain the illusion of an indigenous Arab nation displaced by Zionism.

The turning point came in **1964**, when the Arab League, meeting in Cairo, created the **Palestine Liberation Organization (PLO)**. Its founding charter explicitly called for the *"liberation of Palestine through armed struggle,"* at a time when Israel did not control the West Bank (then annexed by Jordan) or Gaza (administered by Egypt). The PLO's mission was therefore not about reclaiming "occupied territory" — it was about erasing Israel entirely.

Arafat: The Egyptian Revolutionary with No Ties to Palestine

The man who became the face of this new identity, **Yasser Arafat**, was not Palestinian by origin. Born in Cairo in 1929 and educated as a civil engineer at King Fuad University (now Cairo University), Arafat had no ancestral roots in the land he claimed to represent. His rise within the PLO had less to do with local legitimacy and more with **Gamal Abdel Nasser's** vision of Arab unity under Egyptian leadership.

For Nasser, appointing an Egyptian revolutionary rather than a local Arab from Jerusalem or Jaffa ensured control. Arafat's loyalty to Cairo made him the perfect instrument to advance pan-Arab nationalism under the guise of "Palestinian liberation." Charismatic and theatrical, Arafat rebranded himself as the savior of a dispossessed people, concealing his Egyptian background and transforming the PLO into both a propaganda machine and a terror network.

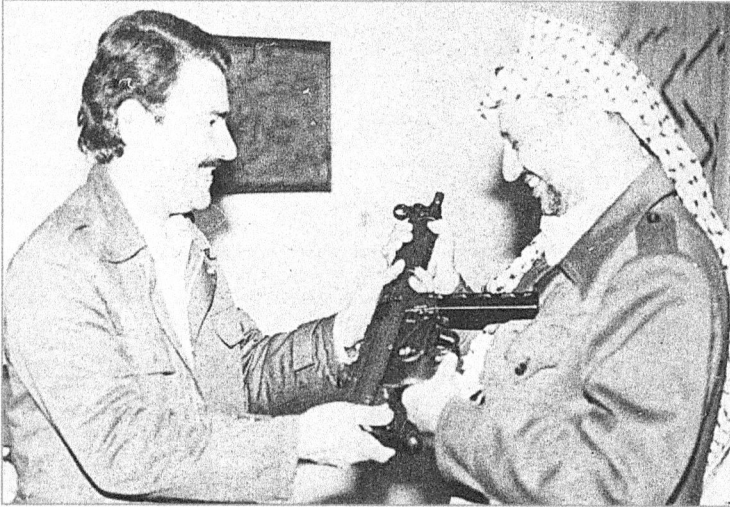

Yasser Arafat (right), February 1980.
Source: Wikimedia Commons / Public Domain.

Arafat understood that to give his new movement legitimacy, it needed more than speeches — it needed recognizable symbols. The next step was to design a flag and visual identity that could create the illusion of an established nation and rally broader Arab support.

The Flag: Borrowed Symbols for a Manufactured Identity

The Palestinian flag, adopted in 1964, is often presented as a timeless emblem of national identity. In reality, it was borrowed directly from the flag of the Arab Revolt against the Ottoman Empire (1916–1918). Its black, white, green, and red colors symbolize **pan-Arab unity**, not a uniquely Palestinian history. The design predated the modern Palestinian movement by half a century and reflected broader Arab nationalist ambitions rather than any indigenous Palestinian heritage.

Historically, the people living in what is now called "Palestine" did not see themselves as a distinct nation. Under Ottoman rule, they were Arabs of southern Syria, loyal to their local clan, village, or tribe — not to a separate Palestinian entity. Even the name "Palestine" was a British administrative term, not a local identity.

Soldiers in the Arab Army during the Arab Revolt of 1916–1918. They are carrying the flag of the Arab Revolt and are pictured in the Arabian Desert
Source: Wikipedia / Public Domain

The adoption of the Arab Revolt flag as the Palestinian flag reinforced this reality: the movement's identity was political, not historical. It was a symbol of convenience — part of a larger Arab strategy to oppose Israel — rather than the emblem of an authentic, long-standing nation.

From Cairo to Terror: The PLO's Transformation

The PLO was created in 1964 under Egyptian supervision, but by the late 1960s it had evolved from a political front into one of the most violent terrorist organizations of the 20th century. After the 1967 Six-Day War — when Israel captured the West Bank and Gaza from Jordan and Egypt — Arafat and his group Fatah took full control of the PLO. Their focus was not on state-building but on internationalizing their war against Israel through terror and propaganda.

117

Between 1968 and 1972, the PLO carried out hundreds of attacks — hijacking airplanes, bombing schools and buses, and murdering Israeli civilians around the world. The 1970 Dawson's Field hijackings in Jordan, the 1972 Lod Airport massacre carried out by the PFLP, and the infamous 1972 Munich Olympics attack, in which 11 Israeli athletes were tortured and murdered, made the PLO a global symbol of terror. These operations were designed not only to kill but to command global attention — to make the "Palestinian cause" impossible to ignore.

Arafat skillfully turned this campaign of violence into political capital. He appeared before the United Nations in 1974 wearing a holster and proclaiming, "I come bearing an olive branch and a freedom fighter's gun." Behind the rhetoric, the PLO's real legacy was bloodshed. Between 1964 and 1972, it killed thousands — Jews, Arabs, Americans, and Europeans alike — while posing as a liberation movement.

The PLO's transformation was complete: born in Cairo as an Arab League creation, it became a global terrorist brand — financed by Soviet weapons, trained by KGB advisers, and sanctified by international media that mistook terror for revolution.

The Soviet Union: The Puppet Masters Behind the PLO

Behind the scenes, much of the PLO's success came from its patrons in Moscow. During the Cold War, the Soviet Union saw the Arab-Israeli conflict as a way to weaken Western influence in the Middle East. Israel was America's ally; the PLO became the Kremlin's proxy.

The KGB and other Soviet intelligence agencies provided the PLO with weapons, funding, intelligence, and training in both guerrilla warfare and disinformation. Soviet instructors trained Arafat and his lieutenants in Lebanon and Eastern Europe, teaching them how to use terrorism not just as violence, but as theater. The PLO's 1968 charter, written in the language of "anti-imperialism" and "national liberation," was lifted almost word-for-word from Soviet ideological manuals.

For Moscow, the "Palestinian cause" was never about justice or self-determination—it was about destabilizing the Middle East, discrediting Israel, and turning the West against its own ally. The Soviets rebranded Israel as a colonial project and the Palestinians as victims of Western imperialism, laying the groundwork for decades of propaganda that still echoes today in universities and international organizations.

By the early 1970s, the PLO had become the perfect Cold War instrument: armed by the Soviets, financed by Arab regimes, sheltered by sympathetic governments, and glorified by much of the world press. What began as an Egyptian-controlled committee in Cairo had evolved into a global network of violence and manipulation—one that would shape the world's perception of the Arab-Israeli conflict for generations to come.

Expelled from Their Hosts: The PLO's Trail of Chaos (1970–1982)

The PLO's campaign of violence didn't just target Israel—it destabilized every country that gave it refuge. Wherever Arafat and his fighters went, bloodshed followed.

After being expelled from Gaza by the Israelis in 1967, the PLO set up base in Jordan. Within three years, its militants had effectively created a "state within a state," challenging King Hussein's authority and terrorizing local civilians. Hijackings, assassinations, and attacks launched from Jordanian soil brought the kingdom to the brink of collapse. In September 1970, after a series of airline hijackings and a failed coup attempt by the PLO, King Hussein finally had enough. He ordered his army to crush the organization. The result was **Black September**—a brutal conflict that left thousands of Palestinians dead and the PLO expelled from Jordan.

Forced out of Jordan, Arafat relocated his headquarters to Lebanon. But instead of seeking stability, the PLO repeated the same pattern. From its new base in Beirut, it launched constant cross-border raids into northern Israel, drawing Israeli retaliations that dragged Lebanon deeper into chaos. By the mid-1970s, the PLO had become a central force in Lebanon's civil war—allying with local militias, running extortion networks, and turning Beirut into its de facto capital. The once-prosperous "Paris of the Middle East" descended into violence and ruin.

Even Arab leaders grew wary. Egypt's Anwar Sadat called Arafat "a professional revolutionary with no loyalty to anyone," and Lebanese Christians accused the PLO of trying to take over their country. By 1982, Israel launched **Operation Peace for Galilee** to drive the PLO out of Lebanon. After a long and costly campaign, Arafat and his fighters were forced to flee once again—this time to Tunis, over 1,500 miles from the land they claimed to "liberate."

The pattern was unmistakable: wherever the PLO went, instability followed. Jordan, Lebanon, and later even Tunisia paid the price for hosting it. The organization that claimed to represent a nation without a homeland left a trail of destruction in every home it occupied.

The PLO: Killing Jews, Muslims and Christians Alike

The PLO's war was never about liberation — it was about domination. Its victims came from every faith and background, united only by their refusal to serve Arafat's political ambitions.

In Israel and abroad, the PLO targeted Jews through terror: plane hijackings, school massacres, and the 1972 Munich Olympics murders that shocked the world. But the organization's violence didn't stop there. In Jordan, it turned its guns on fellow Arabs during *Black September* (1970), killing thousands of Palestinians and Jordanians in an attempt to overthrow King Hussein. In Lebanon, it repeated the pattern, using local communities as human shields and dragging the country into a civil war that claimed hundreds of thousands of lives.

The **Damour massacre of 1976** exposed the full extent of the PLO's barbarity. PLO gunmen entered the Lebanese Christian town, slaughtering entire families — men, women, and children — burning homes, and raping women. Their victims were native Arab Christians who had lived there peacefully for generations. It was not a "resistance" act — it was religious and ethnic cleansing.

These weren't isolated crimes; they revealed the true character of the movement. Whether the victims were Jews in Israel, Muslims in Jordan, or Christians in Lebanon, the PLO's mission was the same: to sow fear, chaos, and division in the name of a fabricated cause. Even Arab leaders learned to fear Arafat's militias, recognizing that wherever they went, destruction followed.

Arafat's Shift to "Moderation" and Missed Peace Opportunities

Over time, Yasser Arafat tried to rebrand himself as a statesman rather than a terrorist. The signing of the Oslo Accords in the 1990s was a turning point, establishing the Palestinian Authority (PA) and granting Palestinians limited self-rule in parts of the West Bank and Gaza. However, Arafat's true intentions remained questionable.

Oslo gave Palestinians control over Gaza and parts of the West Bank, with the promise of final-status negotiations to resolve key issues like borders, refugees, and Jerusalem. Yet, instead of leveraging this progress to secure statehood, the Palestinian leadership faltered. Internal divisions and a failure to rein in violence against Israelis shattered trust. Instead of working within the framework, they allowed the process to collapse, effectively abandoning another chance at sovereignty.

By the time the Camp David Summit of 2000 came around, Israel was prepared to offer unprecedented concessions. Prime Minister Ehud Barak proposed a Palestinian state on 95% of the West Bank and all of Gaza, with land swaps to make up for the remaining territory. The deal included Palestinian sovereignty over Arab neighborhoods in East Jerusalem and a solution to the refugee issue, offering financial compensation and limited resettlement. This was the moment the Palestinians had long claimed to be waiting for—a viable state with its capital in East Jerusalem. And what did Yasser Arafat do? He rejected it outright, without even presenting a counterproposal. Instead, he let the talks collapse, and within months, the Second Intifada erupted, plunging the region into a wave of violence and bloodshed. Arafat's refusal wasn't just a missed opportunity; it was a catastrophic failure of leadership that doomed his people to further suffering.

Yasser Arafat, Ehud Barak, and Bill Clinton at the 2000 Camp David Summit
Source: Sharon Farmer / Wikimedia Commons / Public Domain

In his memoir *My Life*, President Bill Clinton described Ehud Barak's offer at the 2000 Camp David Summit as an extraordinary and unprecedented proposal for peace. Clinton emphasized that Barak's offer addressed nearly all Palestinian demands, yet Yasser Arafat rejected it outright without offering any counterproposal. Clinton expressed deep frustration, stating that Arafat had "missed the opportunity of a lifetime."

He noted that while Barak showed great courage in making such far-reaching concessions, Arafat's unwillingness to compromise derailed the negotiations, leaving Clinton to conclude that the Palestinian leader was never ready to make peace.

If Arafat's rejection of Barak's offer wasn't enough, Mahmoud Abbas's response to Ehud Olmert's 2008 proposal sealed the pattern of Palestinian intransigence. Olmert's plan went even further than Barak's, offering a Palestinian state on 95% of the West Bank, with land swaps for the rest, a land corridor linking Gaza and the West Bank, and shared sovereignty over Jerusalem. It also included an international mechanism to compensate Palestinian refugees. By any measure, this was a historic opportunity. Yet Abbas, like Arafat before him, walked away. He didn't even bother to present a formal counteroffer. The offer was left to gather dust, while the Palestinian leadership continued to bemoan their statelessness without taking meaningful steps to end it.

The pattern is unmistakable. At every major turning point, the Palestinian leadership has chosen rejection over negotiation, clinging to maximalist demands that no Israeli government could ever accept. They have consistently insisted on the "right of return" for millions of descendants of refugees to Israel—a demand that is politically and demographically impossible for Israel to agree to. They have demanded full sovereignty over East Jerusalem, including the Jewish holy sites, while offering nothing in return. Their refusal to engage with even the most generous offers shows that they are not fighting for a state in the West Bank and Gaza—they are holding out for a dream of claiming all of historic Palestine, an aspiration that has long since become a fantasy.

The rejection of these peace offers underscored a persistent pattern: Palestinian leaders prioritized perpetuating the conflict over achieving a viable state. Whether out of fear of losing their grip on power or a refusal to compromise on the "right of return," Arafat and his successors repeatedly sabotaged opportunities for peace.

Palestinian Autonomy: Corruption, Division, and Extremism

Today, the Palestinian Authority (PA) governs parts of the West Bank, but its rule is marred by corruption, authoritarianism, and mismanagement. Billions of dollars in international aid — intended for hospitals, education, and infrastructure — have disappeared into the pockets of officials and their cronies. Transparency International and other watchdogs routinely rank the PA among the most corrupt governing bodies in the world. Meanwhile, ordinary Palestinians face chronic unemployment, decaying infrastructure, and an economy sustained almost entirely by foreign handouts.

Adding to the scandal is the PA's notorious **"Pay for Slay"** policy — a program that provides monthly stipends to Palestinians imprisoned for terrorism and to the families of those killed while attacking Israelis. The more serious the attack, the higher the payout. A terrorist serving a life sentence for murdering civilians can receive several times the average Palestinian wage, funded by foreign aid. This system, enshrined in Palestinian law, turns violence into a career path and martyrdom into an income stream. It not only glorifies terrorism but institutionalizes it, sending a clear message to new generations: killing Israelis pays.

Meanwhile, Gaza remains under the control of **Hamas**, which violently seized power from the PA in 2007. Hamas's Islamist dictatorship has transformed Gaza into a fortified launching pad for rocket attacks, embedding weapons in schools, mosques, and hospitals while its leaders live in luxury. The result is a humanitarian catastrophe entirely of their own making.

The split between the PA and Hamas reflects a deeper truth: Palestinian leadership is not only divided — it is dysfunctional by design. Rather than investing in education, infrastructure, or genuine nation-building, both factions sustain a culture of victimhood and perpetual conflict. For them, peace is a threat — because reconciliation would end the flow of foreign money and the narrative that justifies their power.

The "Right of Return": A Blueprint for Israel's Destruction

Israel is under constant pressure from the UN, the Arab world and even some voices in the U.S. to accept the "right of return" for millions of Palestinians. While it's framed as a humanitarian solution, it's really a political weapon aimed at destroying Israel. The Arab states have kept this issue alive for decades to undermine Israel, and some in the West are buying into the narrative without understanding the catastrophic consequences. Allowing millions of Palestinians to flood Israel isn't about justice—it's about wiping Israel off the map.

Today, approximately 15 million people worldwide identify as Palestinians. The idea of allowing all of them to "return" to Israel is not just a threat—it is an existential catastrophe waiting to happen. Such a move would unleash unparalleled chaos, dismantle the Jewish state, and trigger the greatest massacre in modern history. It is nothing short of a blueprint for annihilation, masquerading as a humanitarian demand.

Israel is home to approximately 10 million people, of which 7.3 million are Jewish. Injecting 15 million Palestinians into this equation would instantly transform Jews into a powerless minority, effectively ending their self-determination in their own homeland. Even if Israel agrees to allow the 6 million descendants of the original 700,000 displaced in 1948 (as estimated by UNRWA) to return, combined with the current Arab population of 2 million, it would result in Jews becoming a minority.

History has shown time and time again what happens when Jews are at the mercy of hostile Muslim majorities. Before 1948, Jews in Arab countries faced systemic persecution, brutal pogroms, forced conversions, and expulsions. Entire Jewish communities were wiped out, their synagogues burned, and their people slaughtered or driven into exile.

Now imagine this scenario playing out again—not in distant lands, but in what is currently the world's only Jewish state. The reality of 15 million

Palestinians overrunning Israel would be a death sentence for its Jewish population. Many Palestinian leaders and factions openly call for Israel's destruction and the imposition of Sharia law, under which Jews would face the same oppression, violence, and persecution they suffered for centuries in Arab lands.

And even if this so-called "return" were restricted to the West Bank and Gaza, the outcome would still be catastrophic. Imagine 7 million Jews surrounded by 15 million Palestinians, many of whom have been indoctrinated to see Jews not as neighbors, but as enemies to be eradicated. The October 7 massacre, when 3,000 Hamas terrorists infiltrated Israel and butchered over 1,200 innocent civilians, was a horrifying glimpse of what could happen. But now, picture 300,000 militants descending on Israel from both Gaza and the West Bank, armed and ready to kill. This would not be a skirmish—it would be a bloodbath of unimaginable proportions, potentially the deadliest massacre in human history.

Chapter 8

The Perpetuation of the Palestinian Problem

The global Palestinian population has grown significantly over the past century. It is estimated today at around **15 millio**n according to the Palestinian Central Bureau of Statistics. This figure includes Palestinians living in the West Bank, Gaza Strip, East Jerusalem, Israel, and the global diaspora. However, the 1922 British Mandate Census recorded only **590,890 Muslims** in Palestine.

The average population growth in the West Bank and Gaza between 1948 and today is around **2%**, according to historical estimates and demographic data from the World Bank, World Population Review, and the United Nations Population Division.

If the 1922 population grew at a steady 2% annual rate, the global Palestinian population today would be around **4.4 million**.

Since the actual estimated global Palestinian population in 2025 is approximately **15 million,** this creates a significant discrepancy between the projected population of **4.4 million** (based on 2% growth) and the actual population, which is more than **three times higher**!

So how did we get here? The numbers don't add up. If anything, the early 1900s' slow growth rates should have further suppressed the overall population trajectory. Instead, we are left grappling with an unexplained leap that defies historical norms and statistical logic. This glaring inconsistency raises an uncomfortable question: who benefits from inflating these figures, and why?

The answer lies not in natural population growth, but in political manipulation. The extraordinary inflation of Palestinian population figures is not an accident—it's the result of deliberate policies designed to preserve victimhood as a permanent status. No other refugee group in modern history has been treated this way. Rather than working toward integration or resettlement, Arab governments and international institutions—chief among them the United Nations—chose to freeze the Palestinians in time, generation after generation. What began as a humanitarian mission slowly evolved into a political weapon. And at the center of this machinery stands one organization: UNRWA.

Critiquing the Role of the UN and the Arab World

The United Nations has two agencies that focus exclusively on refugees: **UNHCR** and **UNRWA**. While both aim to provide aid and protection, their approaches are fundamentally different. UNHCR is responsible for all refugees worldwide, helping them find permanent solutions, such as resettlement or integration. UNRWA, on the other hand, focuses solely on Palestinian refugees, taking a unique approach that perpetuates their refugee status indefinitely. This distinction has led to significant criticism of UNRWA for creating a situation unlike any other in the world.

UNHCR, the United Nations High Commissioner for Refugees, was created in 1950 to deal with the massive displacement caused by World War II. Its mission is clear: to protect refugees and help them rebuild their lives by either integrating them into their host countries, resettling them in third countries, or supporting their return to their home countries when safe.

Over the years, UNHCR has handled some of the largest refugee crises in history:

- **Syrian Civil War**: Since 2011, more than 6.8 million Syrians have become refugees, mostly living in countries like Turkey, Lebanon, and Jordan. UNHCR works to provide housing, education, and legal status for these individuals.

- **Afghan Refugees**: Decades of conflict have displaced 2.6 million Afghan refugees, many of whom now live in Iran and Pakistan. UNHCR facilitates repatriation when possible and advocates for their resettlement.
- **Ukraine Conflict**: Following the 2022 Russian invasion, over 6 million of Ukrainians fled to neighboring countries. UNHCR has coordinated humanitarian aid, legal support, and temporary housing.
- **Myanmar**: Over 1 million Rohingya Muslims fled violence in Myanmar to Bangladesh since 2017.
- **Rwandan Genocide**: Over 2 million refugees fled to neighboring countries like Zaire (now the Democratic Republic of Congo), Uganda, and Tanzania since 1994.
- **Vietnam War and Southeast Asia (1955–1975)**: More than 3 million refugees, including the "boat people" who fled Vietnam, Laos, and Cambodia after the fall of Saigon.
- **Korean War (1950–1953)**: Millions of Koreans fled violence, with large-scale displacement within South Korea and into neighboring countries.
- **World War II (post-1945)**: Over 20 million of Europeans displaced by the war

UNHCR works toward reducing the number of refugees by finding them permanent solutions.

In contrast, **UNRWA**, the United Nations Relief and Works Agency for Palestine Refugees, operates differently. It was established in 1949 specifically for the 700,000 Palestinians displaced by the 1948 Arab-Israeli War. Unlike UNHCR, UNRWA does not focus on resettling refugees or integrating them into host countries. Instead, it provides services like education, healthcare, and housing assistance, but it also allows refugee status to **pass down through generations**.

This policy is unique to Palestinian refugees. Today, UNRWA serves **5.9 million** Palestinian refugees, nearly all of whom are descendants of the original 700,000 displaced in 1948. No other refugee group in the world is treated this way. For example:

- A Syrian refugee's child born in Turkey is no longer considered a refugee if they integrate into Turkish society.
- A Ukrainian refugee resettled in Europe is no longer considered a refugee once they receive citizenship or permanent residency.

Palestinians are the most privileged refugees in the world. Even those who were born or acquired citizenship in countries like Jordan—are still counted as refugees. This creates a growing population of refugees, with no end in sight.

The key difference between UNHCR and UNRWA lies in their goals. UNHCR works to solve refugee crises, while UNRWA sustains one. By allowing refugee status to pass between generations and focusing exclusively on Palestinians, UNRWA has created a unique, unsustainable situation.

The Double Standard

Why are Palestinians treated differently from Syrians, Afghans, or Ukrainians? Why the Double Standard?

One major reason UNRWA continues is money. The agency operates on a yearly budget of about $1.6 billion, which comes from donations made by countries such as the United States and members of the European Union. These funds not only go to supporting descendants of the 1948 refugees but also create jobs for over 28,000 employees. UNRWA is one of the largest employers in Palestinian territories, Lebanon, and Jordan, and its spending provides a boost to local economies.

The economic impact of UNRWA extends beyond just the refugees it serves. For host countries, UNRWA's presence means they don't have to integrate Palestinians fully or provide them with the same rights and services as citizens. In Lebanon, for instance, Palestinian refugees are not allowed to own property or work in certain professions, which keeps them reliant on UNRWA. This dependency creates a system where neither the refugees nor the host countries push for permanent solutions, keeping the cycle going.

On the political side, UNRWA's existence helps keep the Palestinian "right of return" alive. No other group of refugees in the world except for Palestinians has their status passed down through generations. For example, Syrian refugees in Turkey are not considered refugees once they integrate or receive citizenship. But in the case of Palestinians, even those who have lived in stable countries like Jordan for decades and have citizenship are still labeled as refugees.

This policy serves political purposes. Many Arab and Muslim countries support UNRWA because it keeps pressure on Israel by maintaining the refugee issue unresolved. These countries often use the refugee narrative as a way to oppose Jewish claims to Jerusalem, especially the Al-Aqsa Mosque. Jerusalem is a focal point for the Muslim world, and UNRWA indirectly helps to strengthen Palestinian claims to the city by keeping the refugee crisis alive.

At the United Nations, Arab and Muslim countries, along with their allies in Africa and Asia, form a majority that consistently votes to renew UNRWA's mandate. These countries use their influence to ensure that the refugee issue remains central to international discussions about the Israeli-Palestinian conflict. For them, UNRWA is not just a humanitarian agency but also a political tool to keep the right of return on the table and prevent the normalization of Israel's sovereignty over Jerusalem.

UNRWA: Spreading Hate and Fueling Conflict

UNRWA's schools are perhaps the most troubling aspect of its operations. UNRWA operates hundreds of schools in the West Bank, Gaza Strip, Lebanon, Jordan, and Syria, educating over half a million Palestinian children. Far from teaching coexistence or peace, these schools promote a narrative of hatred and violence. Textbooks glorify individuals like Dalal Mughrabi, who led a 1978 terror attack that killed 38 Israelis, including children. Maps in classrooms erase Israel entirely, labeling the entire region as "Palestine." Students are taught that martyrdom is a noble goal, and math problems even incorporate violent imagery, such as counting the number of "martyrs" in battles.

These lessons are not just theoretical; they shape generations of Palestinian youth to see violence as the only solution. This indoctrination ensures the conflict continues, with new generations primed to embrace extremism.

In addition to glorifying violence, the textbooks frequently erase the existence of Israel. Maps used in UNRWA schools often label the entire region as "Palestine," with no mention of Israel at all. This practice not only denies Israel's legitimacy but also reinforces the idea that the Jewish state should not exist. Furthermore, some educational materials describe Jews in negative stereotypes, portraying them as oppressors or occupiers in ways that fuel antisemitism among young students.

Investigations by organizations like the **Institute for Monitoring Peace and Cultural Tolerance in School Education (IMPACT-se)** have documented these issues extensively. Despite promises from UNRWA to review and address problematic content, nothing has been done to remove such materials. Moreover, UNRWA teachers and staff have also been accused of sharing inflammatory content on social media, including posts that glorify terrorism and call for violence against Jews.

Following the October 7 attack on southern Israel, UNRWA has faced intense criticism. A UN investigation found that nine UNRWA staff members were involved in the attack. Israeli officials accused even more, claiming 12 staff members took active part directly, with others linked to groups like Hamas or Islamic Jihad.

UNRWA: A Political Weapon Disguised as Humanitarian Aid

UNRWA's existence serves the broader political goals of the Muslim world, which seeks to weaken Israel and maintain control over Jerusalem, particularly the Al-Aqsa Mosque. By keeping the refugee crisis alive, these nations use UNRWA as a tool to delegitimize Israel's sovereignty and block any resolution to the conflict. At the United Nations, Muslim-majority countries consistently support UNRWA's mandate. This majority ensures that the agency remains untouchable, regardless of its blatant failures and ties to extremism.

UNRWA is not a humanitarian organization—it is a political weapon. Its policies perpetuate a refugee crisis that should have been resolved decades ago, and its operations directly fuel hatred and violence. The international community must stop funding this agency and demand real solutions for Palestinians. Refugees should be resettled, integrated into host countries, or given new opportunities to rebuild their lives—not used as pawns in a political game against Israel. Until UNRWA is dismantled, it will remain a barrier to peace and a supporter of extremism in the region.

The UN's Bias Against Israel: A Modern-Day Obsession

The United Nations, an institution built on ideals of fairness and equality, has become a breeding ground for relentless, one-sided attacks on Israel—a democratic state in the Middle East. Let's call it what it is: **institutionalized antisemitism**. While Israel is held to impossible standards and vilified in hundreds of resolutions, some of the world's most oppressive regimes walk away unscathed, their crimes ignored or excused. The result is a moral inversion where the only Jewish state is treated as a global pariah, while dictators and human rights abusers sit in judgment.

A Numbers Game: The UN's Obsession with Israel

The numbers speak volumes. Since its founding, the UN has passed hundreds of resolutions targeting Israel, often ignoring the broader complexities of the Middle East or the hostile provocations Israel faces daily.

- From 2015 to 2022, the General Assembly adopted 140 resolutions criticizing Israel, compared to just 68 resolutions addressing all other countries combined. That's right: a nation about the size of New Jersey gets condemned more than the entire rest of the world.

- The UN Human Rights Council (UNHRC) has passed over 90 resolutions against Israel since 2006. For context, Syria, which has slaughtered hundreds of thousands in a brutal civil war, has faced fewer resolutions. Iran, a state sponsor of terrorism that brutally suppresses its own people, receives only a fraction of the criticism.

The Real Hypocrisy: Ignoring the Worst Offenders

While the United Nations spends an extraordinary amount of time condemning Israel, some of the world's most repressive regimes operate with near impunity. It's a moral inversion on a global scale: the world's only Jewish democracy, and the Middle East's only democracy, is treated as the world's greatest violator of human rights, while genuine tyrannies receive token criticism or even seats on human rights councils.

- **North Korea:** The UN's own investigators have described North Korea's network of prison camps as a system of "crimes against humanity." Hundreds of thousands of men, women, and children are enslaved in forced labor camps, starved, and tortured. Yet from 2015 to 2020, the UN General Assembly passed only **six** resolutions condemning Pyongyang — one per year. Israel, by comparison, faced more than **100** condemnations in the same timeframe.

- **Iran:** The Iranian regime publicly calls for Israel's destruction while brutally oppressing its own citizens. Women are beaten for refusing to wear the hijab; protesters are shot in the streets; and LGBTQ+ people face imprisonment or execution. Between 2015 and 2020, the UNGA passed **six** resolutions against Iran — again, one per year — while Iran sat on various UN committees, including the Commission on the Status of Women. The irony is grotesque: a regime that stones women to death for "immorality" lectures Israel on human rights.

- **Syria:** Under Bashar al-Assad, Syria has committed war crimes on an industrial scale: gassing civilians with chemical weapons, starving besieged towns, and bombing hospitals. More than half a million people have been killed. Between 2015 and 2020, the UN Security Council managed to pass just **eight** resolutions related to Syria — most of them symbolic due to Russian and Chinese vetoes. Meanwhile, Israel — a country that rescues Syrian war victims across its border — remains the UN's favorite target.

- **China:** The Chinese Communist Party operates the largest network of concentration camps since World War II. Over a million Uyghur Muslims have been detained in "reeducation" centers; others are subjected to forced sterilizations and labor. The UN has yet to pass a single General Assembly resolution directly condemning China for these abuses. When Western nations tried to table one in 2022, it failed — blocked by a coalition of authoritarian states and their allies on the UN Human Rights Council.

- **Russia:** Russia's annexation of Crimea, its bombing of civilians in Syria, and its invasion of Ukraine are all flagrant violations of international law. Yet between 2015 and 2020, the UN General Assembly passed only a handful of resolutions condemning Moscow. Even after the invasion of Ukraine in 2022, Russia continued to sit on UN committees, including those overseeing disarmament.

- **Myanmar:** In 2017, Myanmar's military carried out a genocidal campaign against the Rohingya Muslim minority — burning villages, killing thousands, and displacing more than a million people. While the UN issued statements and limited sanctions, it took years before even symbolic resolutions appeared. The generals who orchestrated the massacres still enjoy freedom, while Israel is condemned for building homes in its own capital.

- **Saudi Arabia:** A monarchy that only recently allowed women to drive, where dissidents are imprisoned or executed, and where public beheadings are a weekly spectacle. Yet Saudi Arabia has repeatedly been elected to the UN Human Rights Council. The same institution that obsesses over Israel's "occupation" has nothing to say about Saudi Arabia's total lack of democratic rights.

The Permanent Agenda Item: A Badge of Hypocrisy

Israel is the **only country in the world to have a dedicated permanent agenda item** at the UNHRC (Item 7). Every session, the council discusses "The human rights situation in Palestine," ensuring that Israel is perpetually under the microscope. Not even the worst regimes on Earth are subjected to this kind of obsessive scrutiny.

What about Hamas, which uses Palestinian civilians as human shields, launches rockets indiscriminately at Israeli cities, and openly calls for genocide? The UN rarely condemns these terrorists with the same fervor it reserves for Israel.

UNESCO and Historical Erasure

Even cultural UN institutions like UNESCO have joined the anti-Israel campaign. Resolutions have been passed denying Jewish ties to the Temple Mount and other sacred sites. In October 2016, UNESCO passed a resolution that erased the 3,000-year Jewish connection to the Temple Mount by exclusively referring to it by its Islamic name, "Al-Haram al-

Sharif". The resolution accused Israel of "aggressions" at the site, portraying Jewish visits as violations, while ignoring the Temple Mount's significance as the holiest site in Judaism. By denying Jewish ties to these sacred places, UNESCO effectively engaged in historical revisionism, pushing a politically motivated, antisemitic agenda to delegitimize Israel's connection to Jerusalem.

The Real Agenda: Delegitimizing Israel

The UN's obsession with Israel isn't about justice or human rights. It's about delegitimization. It's about singling out the world's only Jewish state for vilification, while ignoring the crimes of despotic regimes. This is nothing less than modern-day antisemitism, dressed up as concern for Palestinians. If the UN cared about Palestinian lives, it would also hold Hamas accountable for war crimes and corruption, and it would push for peace rather than demonization.

The Muslim Majority: A Voting Bloc with an Agenda

A significant driver of this bias is the sheer size and influence of the Muslim-majority countries within the UN. The **Organization of Islamic Cooperation (OIC)**, a bloc of 57 member states (the largest voting bloc in the UN), has an explicit political agenda to isolate Israel. Many of these countries refuse to recognize Israel's right to exist and use their collective influence to push through resolutions condemning the Jewish state. For example:

- The OIC consistently sponsors anti-Israel resolutions and ensures that Israel remains a permanent agenda item at the UNHRC (Item 7).
- Votes against Israel often pass overwhelmingly because OIC nations align with other blocs like the **Non-Aligned Movement (NAM)** to secure a majority.

This bloc politics ensures that Israel is outvoted on nearly every resolution, regardless of the merits of the case or the broader context.

Political Opportunism: Why the World Joins In

Beyond the Muslim-majority nations, other countries often align with anti-Israel resolutions for political convenience. Supporting anti-Israel measures costs them nothing but garners goodwill with influential OIC nations, particularly in economic and diplomatic spheres. Voting against Israel becomes a political bargaining chip:

- **European nations**, eager to maintain trade relationships with oil-rich Middle Eastern countries, often turn a blind eye to the UN's bias against Israel.
- **Developing countries**, reliant on financial aid or investments from OIC nations, align with anti-Israel rhetoric to curry favor.

This political opportunism fuels a self-perpetuating cycle where Israel is condemned, not for its actions, but as part of a broader geopolitical game.

Time to Call Out the UN

The UN's bias against Israel isn't accidental — it's built into the system. For decades, bloc voting by Muslim-majority nations and Cold War politics have turned the organization's founding ideals upside down. Instead of defending human rights, the UN has become a stage where dictatorships deflect attention from their own crimes by demonizing the world's only Jewish democracy.

A major driver of this distortion is the **Organization of Islamic Cooperation (OIC)** — 57 nations that coordinate to pass automatic anti-Israel resolutions. The UN Human Rights Council even has a standing **Agenda Item 7**, dedicated exclusively to condemning Israel. No other nation on earth is treated this way.

Meanwhile, serial human rights violators like Iran, China, and Cuba routinely sit on the same UN councils that condemn Israel. Saudi Arabia has even chaired a panel for human rights appointments. The hypocrisy would be laughable if it weren't so destructive.

Israel stands out in the Middle East as a democracy with free elections, a free press, and equal rights for Jews, Muslims, and Christians alike — yet it remains the UN's favorite target. This obsession has nothing to do with peace or justice; it's about politics, power blocs, and antisemitism dressed up as diplomacy.

If the UN wants to regain its moral credibility, it must end its double standard, hold all nations equally accountable, and stop turning the world's only Jewish state into its permanent scapegoat.

Chapter 9

The Rising of Hamas

Hamas, an acronym for Harakat al-Muqawamah al-Islamiyya (Islamic Resistance Movement), emerged as a significant force in the Palestinian territories during the late 1980s. Founded in 1987 as an offshoot of the Muslim Brotherhood, Hamas initially portrayed itself as a social and political movement aimed at resisting Israeli occupation and promoting Islamic values. However, it quickly evolved into one of the most influential and feared terrorist organizations in the world, known for its unrelenting violence, oppressive governance, and radical Islamist agenda.

The Origins of Hamas: From Charity to Terror

Hamas was born during the First Intifada, a Palestinian uprising against Israeli rule in the West Bank and Gaza. It differentiated itself from the secular Palestine Liberation Organization (PLO) by emphasizing its Islamist roots and its goal of establishing an Islamic state in all of historic Palestine. Its foundational document, the Hamas Charter, published in 1988, provides chilling insight into its ideology.

Key excerpts from the charter include:

- **Article 7**: "The Day of Judgment will not come until Muslims fight the Jews and kill them; when the Jew will hide behind stones and trees, the stones and trees will say, 'O Muslim, O Servant of Allah, there is a Jew behind me, come and kill him.'"

- **Article 13**: "There is no solution for the Palestinian question except through Jihad."

From its inception, Hamas rejected any peaceful resolution to the Israeli-Palestinian conflict, framing itself as a vanguard of militant resistance.

The Bloody Coup: Hamas's Rise to Power

Hamas entered the political arena in 2006, winning a surprising majority in the Palestinian Legislative Council elections. This victory set the stage for a violent confrontation with the Palestinian Authority (PA).

In 2007, Hamas carried out a brutal coup in Gaza, ousting the PA in a conflict that left hundreds dead. The methods employed during this takeover were particularly brutal. Reports described Hamas fighters dragging suspected PA supporters into the streets, executing them publicly, and throwing others off rooftops. The scenes of terror signaled the beginning of Hamas's iron-fisted rule over Gaza.

After the violent coup, Hamas took full control of the Gaza Strip, wiping out any trace of the Palestinian Authority's presence. Since **Israel completely pulled out of Gaza in 2005**, there hasn't been a single Israeli soldier or civilian in the area. All settlements were dismantled, and the territory was handed over entirely to Palestinian control. Since then, Hamas has ruled Gaza with an iron grip.

A Reign of Oppression

Under Hamas's rule, Gaza has become a living nightmare for many of its residents. The regime enforces strict Islamic law and ruthlessly suppresses dissent.

- **Persecution of Opponents**: Political opponents, journalists, and activists face arbitrary arrests, torture, and execution. Dissent is not tolerated, creating a climate of fear that permeates every aspect of life in Gaza.
- **Oppression of Women**: Women live under severe restrictions. They are subject to mandatory dress codes, limited educational and professional opportunities, and systemic inequality. Hamas enforces these rules with a moral police force that ensures compliance with its interpretation of Sharia law.

- **Persecution of LGBTQ+ Individuals**: Hamas's treatment of LGBTQ+ individuals is particularly egregious. Being openly gay in Gaza can result in imprisonment, torture, or even execution. Human rights groups have documented horrifying cases of abuse against LGBTQ+ individuals, some of whom are forced to flee Gaza to survive.

The Indoctrination of Children

One of the most disturbing aspects of Hamas's rule is its systematic indoctrination of children. Through schools, media, and summer camps, Hamas instills its radical ideology in young minds. Children are often taught to glorify "martyrs" who die carrying out attacks on Israelis. Summer camps run by Hamas train tens of thousands of boys in military tactics, including the use of weapons and combat maneuvers, conditioning them for future conflict.

Hamas military training for children
Source: Hadi Mohammad / Fars Media Corporation / Wikimedia Commons / CC BY 4.0

A 2016 report detailed how over **25,000** children attended Hamas's summer camps, where activities included crawling under barbed wire, dismantling mock explosives, and chanting slogans calling for the destruction of Israel. These camps are not about recreation; they are designed to produce the next generation of terrorists.

A History of Terror

Hamas's reputation as a terrorist organization was cemented through decades of attacks on Israeli civilians.

- **Suicide Bombings**: During the Second Intifada (2000–2005), Hamas conducted more than **60 suicide bombings**, killing over 1,000 Israelis and injuring over 8,000. These attacks targeted buses, cafes, shopping malls, and even Passover seders, leaving a trail of death and destruction. The Intifada was fueled by a rejection of the Oslo Accords and Israel's generous peace offers, as Palestinian leaders insisted on demands like the "right of return" for millions of refugee descendants and opposed Jewish worship at holy sites in Jerusalem.

- **Rocket Attacks**: Since 2001, Hamas has launched over **30,000 rockets** at Israeli towns and cities, indiscriminately targeting civilian populations. In 2014 alone, 4,500 rockets were fired, forcing millions of Israelis into bomb shelters. During the May 2021 conflict, over 4,300 rockets were launched in just 11 days. In the 2023 War in Gaza, Hamas fired over 13,000 rockets—5,000 of them on October 7.

- **October 7, 2023 Massacre**: Hamas launched the deadliest attack against Jews since the Holocaust. Under the guise of rocket fire, over 3,000 heavily armed terrorists breached Israel's borders, storming civilian communities. The attackers unleashed unspeakable brutality—raping women, beheading civilians, and burning people alive in their own homes. In a single day, over 1,200 Israelis were massacred, with thousands more injured or kidnapped.

Exploitation of Resources

Hamas's governance in Gaza has been marked by corruption and exploitation. While much of Gaza's population lives in poverty, Hamas leaders live in luxury abroad.

- **Misuse of Aid**: Billions of dollars in international aid intended for Gaza's humanitarian relief have been siphoned off to fund Hamas's military wing. This includes constructing elaborate networks of terror tunnels and amassing weapons stockpiles.
- **Leaders' Wealth**: Hamas leaders, such as Khaled Mashal, are known to reside in luxury in Qatar, with personal fortunes reportedly exceeding $2 billion. This stark contrast between the leaders' wealth and Gaza's poverty highlights the extent of Hamas's corruption.

The Blockade and Humanitarian Aid

Hamas often blames Gaza's economic hardships on the Israeli blockade. However, this narrative ignores several crucial facts:

- Israel enforces the blockade to prevent Hamas from smuggling weapons and materials used for terrorism.
- Despite ongoing attacks, Israel has allowed billions of dollars in aid to flow into Gaza, provided electricity and water, and issued work permits to tens of thousands of Gazans.
- In contrast, Egypt, which also borders Gaza, has imposed stricter restrictions and offered far less aid.

Iranian Sponsorship

Hamas's ability to wage war and sustain its brutal control over Gaza is deeply tied to its primary benefactor, Iran. Often called the world's foremost state sponsor of terrorism, Iran funnels money, weapons, and strategic support to Hamas, seeing it as a critical piece in its geopolitical strategy. This strategy, commonly referred to as the "Axis of Resistance," includes Iran, Syria, Yamen, Hezbollah in Lebanon, and a range of smaller militant groups across the Middle East. Together, they form a dangerous network dedicated to countering Western influence, spreading Islamist extremism, and, above all, destroying Israel.

Iran doesn't just support Hamas for ideological reasons. It views the group as a convenient proxy to destabilize the region and strike at Israel without risking direct conflict. By empowering Hamas, Iran amplifies its influence far beyond its borders, creating chaos while avoiding the consequences of its actions. The regime's hand is evident in nearly every missile launched from Gaza and every tunnel dug beneath its borders.

The Role of Hezbollah in the Axis of Resistance

A key ally in this network is **Hezbollah**, a militant group based in Lebanon that operates with similar goals to Hamas. Backed by billions of dollars from Iran, Hezbollah grew into a formidable military force, with an arsenal of over 150,000 rockets pointed at Israel. Hezbollah and Hamas often coordinated their activities, leveraging their shared hatred of Israel to spread terror. This partnership reflects the broader strategy of the Axis of Resistance: to surround Israel with hostile forces on multiple fronts.

Iran's Supreme Leader **Ayatollah Ali Khamenei** has openly declared Hamas an essential part of Tehran's "Axis of Resistance." *"The fight against Israel is a public duty for all Muslims,"* he proclaimed in 2021, framing Hamas's war against Israel as a religious obligation. Khamenei has repeatedly called for Israel's destruction, describing it as a *"cancerous tumor that must be removed."*

For Iran, Hamas is not about Palestinian liberation but regional domination. Backed with Iranian funding, weapons, and training, Hamas serves as Tehran's proxy in Gaza—just as Hezbollah does in Lebanon and the Houthis in Yemen.

The Dark Reality Behind Iran's Sponsorship

While Iran positions itself as a champion of the Palestinian people, its own record of human rights abuses exposes the hypocrisy of this narrative. The regime's brutal oppression of its own citizens is a stark reminder of what Hamas, as Iran's ally, truly represents.

Women in Iran are among the most visible victims of the regime's cruelty. Legally required to wear hijab in public, women face harsh punishments, including imprisonment, for defying the government's strict dress codes. The death of Mahsa Amini in 2022, after she was beaten by Iran's so-called "morality police" for wearing her hijab improperly, sparked global outrage. This young woman's murder highlighted the systemic violence women endure under Iranian rule, where even basic freedoms are stripped away.

LGBTQ+ individuals face even worse treatment. Homosexuality in Iran is punishable by death, and the regime's methods are as barbaric as they are terrifying. Public hangings, secret executions, and forced confessions are common. Iranian leaders openly celebrate these atrocities, calling them a defense of morality. The message is clear: dissent, diversity, and individual freedoms have no place in Iran's vision of society.

The Iranian government's oppressive tactics extend far beyond women and LGBTQ+ communities. Political dissenters, journalists, and activists are routinely arrested, tortured, and executed. In 2022 alone, over 500 protesters were killed as Iranians took to the streets to demand basic rights. This is the regime that funds and arms Hamas—a regime that shares the same authoritarian, violent, and radical worldview.

Hamas and Iran: A Partnership in Terror

Iran's support for Hamas goes far beyond money. It has provided Hamas with the technology and training to manufacture advanced weaponry in Gaza. With Iran's help, Hamas has built rockets capable of reaching Israeli cities like Tel Aviv and Jerusalem. These weapons are often constructed in underground facilities, shielded from detection, thanks to Iranian expertise.

IDF Soldiers Near Confiscated Badr-3 Hamas Rockets in Gaza, November 2023
Source: IDF Spokesperson's Unit / Wikimedia Commons / CC BY-SA 3.0

The infamous tunnel networks under Gaza—used for smuggling, storing weapons, and launching attacks—are another product of Iranian support. Often called the "Gaza Metro," these tunnels are a testament to the scale of resources Iran has poured into Hamas's military operations. These aren't defensive measures; they are tools of terror, built at the expense of Gaza's civilians.

The Hypocrisy of Pro-Hamas Supporters

It is critical to understand what supporting Hamas truly means. Those who rally behind the group, claiming to stand for Palestinian rights, are, in fact, endorsing the murderous ideology of Iran. By aligning with Hamas, these supporters are tacitly supporting the oppression of women, the persecution of LGBTQ+ individuals, and the systematic violence against political dissenters—all hallmarks of the Iranian regime.

Moreover, by backing Hamas, they are complicit in perpetuating a cycle of violence that has devastated the lives of Palestinians. Iranian money doesn't build schools or hospitals in Gaza—it builds rockets and tunnels. It doesn't fund relief efforts—it funds terror. The suffering of Gaza's people is not the result of Israeli policies alone but of Hamas's decision to prioritize war over welfare, guided and funded by Iran.

A Partnership Built on Oppression

The relationship between Hamas and Iran is a marriage of convenience between two entities that thrive on oppression and violence. For Hamas, Iranian support provides the resources needed to sustain its war against Israel. For Iran, Hamas is a tool to spread chaos and advance its agenda. But for the people of Gaza, this partnership has brought nothing but suffering. Instead of aid, they receive weapons. Instead of development, they get tunnels. Instead of hope, they are given endless war.

Iran's sponsorship of Hamas reveals the true nature of both organizations: they are not defenders of the Palestinian people or their rights. They are architects of terror, driven by a shared commitment to radical ideology and the destruction of their enemies. Recognizing this reality is crucial to understanding the broader dynamics of the conflict and the forces that perpetuate it.

Chapter 10

October 7 and the War in Gaza

On October 7, 2023, Israel was plunged into darkness. Hamas launched an unprovoked and unprecedented attack on Israeli civilians. Under the guise of rocket fire, over 3,000 heavily armed terrorists breached Israel's borders, storming civilian communities with the sole intent to murder, mutilate, and terrorize. Entire families were slaughtered in their homes; parents were executed in front of their children, and children were executed in front of their parents. The attackers unleashed unspeakable brutality—raping women, beheading civilians, and burning people alive in their own homes

The assault began with a massacre at the Nova Music Festival, where thousands of young people gathered to celebrate life and music. Armed Hamas terrorists stormed the festival, killing over 260 attendees in cold blood. Survivors recount harrowing scenes: women dragged away to be raped and murdered, bodies mutilated beyond recognition, and families gunned down while trying to flee.

The atrocities extended beyond the festival grounds. In southern Israeli towns near the Gaza border, entire families were executed in their homes. Parents and children were burned alive. Infants were slaughtered in their cribs. The brutality was unimaginable. Over 1,200 Israelis were murdered in a single day—the highest death toll in Israel's history. Thousands more were injured or taken hostage, including children, women, and the elderly.

The atrocities did not stop with the killings. Hamas terrorists desecrated bodies, parading them through the streets of Gaza as crowds cheered. Elderly Holocaust survivors were dragged from their homes and abducted, an unfathomable echo of the horrors they had endured decades earlier. Children and infants were taken hostage, and entire kibbutzim were razed to the ground. These acts, fueled by sheer hatred, represent a level of inhumanity that shocked the world. This was not a political statement or an isolated attack; it was a deliberate effort to erase Jewish lives, culture, and humanity.

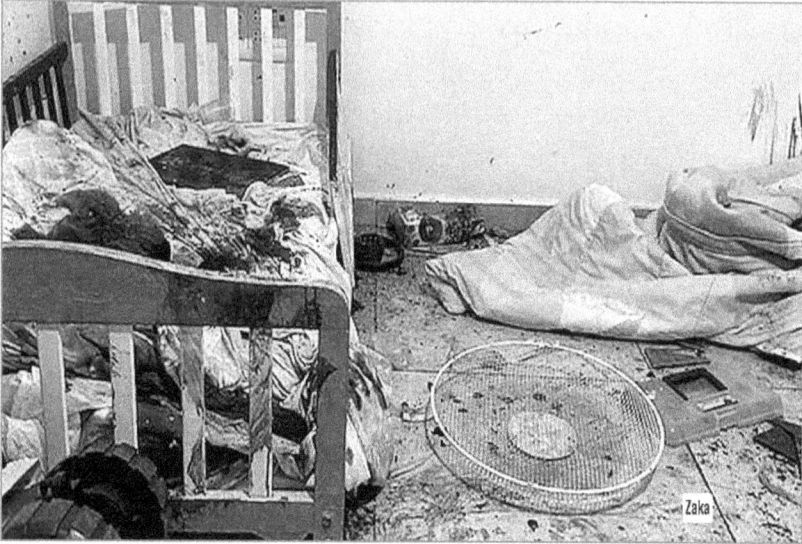

Aftermath of the October 7 Hamas Attack: Blood-Stained Crib and Ravaged Room
Source: Spokesperson Unit of ZAKA / Wikimedia Commons / CC BY-SA 4.0

Before the unimaginable horrors of October 7, Israel endured decades of relentless attacks targeting its civilian population. Suicide bombings in buses, cafes, and marketplaces left streets soaked in blood, turning ordinary days into scenes of chaos and carnage. In the Second Intifada alone, over 1,000 Israelis—men, women, and children—were murdered in cold blood. Hamas, Islamic Jihad, and other terrorist groups launched thousands of rockets, indiscriminately raining death on homes, schools, and kindergartens. Each attack was a calculated act of terror, designed not only to kill but to shatter lives and instill fear.

Israel, like any sovereign nation, has the right and duty to defend its citizens. What nation would tolerate its people being butchered and abducted?

Hamas: A Terror Regime Built on Civilian Suffering

Hamas's strategy is not just cruel; it's deliberate. This terrorist organization operates by embedding itself within Gaza's civilian population, using them as human shields. Their fighters wear civilian clothes, making it nearly impossible to distinguish them from non-combatants. Weapons, including RPGs and rifles, are hidden in homes, mosques, and schools. Underneath Gaza lies an extensive network of terror tunnels, stretching for over 300 miles—longer than the London Underground. These tunnels are not designed to protect Gaza's civilians but to smuggle weapons, transport fighters, and plan attacks on Israel.

What makes this even more horrifying is how Hamas has used billions of dollars in international aid. Instead of building schools, hospitals, or infrastructure to improve the lives of Gazans, they've built a terror state. The aid has gone into stockpiling weapons, constructing terror tunnels, and manufacturing rockets, all while Gaza's civilians are left to live in poverty and despair.

The Tragedy of Human Shields and Inflated Casualties

Hamas's use of human shields is not a byproduct of urban warfare; it is their core strategy. They fire rockets from residential buildings, use hospitals as command centers, and store weapons in schools. When Israel responds to these threats, civilian casualties are tragic but inevitable. Israel's military, unlike Hamas, takes extraordinary steps to minimize civilian harm. The "knock on the roof" procedure is a prime example: before striking a building used by Hamas, Israel drops non-lethal munitions or sends warnings to give civilians time to evacuate. This level of precaution is unheard of in modern warfare.

Yet Hamas prevents civilians from fleeing to safety. When Israel urged northern Gaza residents to evacuate to avoid harm, Hamas militants threatened and even shot those attempting to leave. Civilians are not just caught in the crossfire—they are held hostage by Hamas's policies.

Claims of mass civilian casualties are further inflated by Hamas, which controls the flow of information from Gaza. Their casualty figures often count Hamas fighters as civilians. They also include teens, who are used as child soldiers by Hamas, under the category of "children." This is not to deny the tragedy of civilian deaths but to highlight that these numbers are manipulated to serve Hamas's propaganda goals.

The Reality of Civilian Casualties

In urban warfare, civilian casualties are unfortunately high, but Israel's ratio of civilians to combatants killed is among the lowest in history for such conflicts. For comparison, during the **2017 Battle of Mosul** in Iraq, coalition forces of the U.S., UK, and Jordan faced similar challenges fighting ISIS in a densely populated city. Civilian-to-combatant ratio in that battle was significantly higher than in Gaza, despite similar urban density. Israel's efforts to minimize harm—including targeting only verified Hamas assets and pausing operations to allow humanitarian aid—are unparalleled.

Israel also allowed daily humanitarian aid into Gaza, ensuring the flow of food, water, and medical supplies. Yet Hamas routinely intercepted and robbed these aid convoys, redirecting supplies to its fighters or selling them at inflated prices. This theft underscores Hamas's indifference to the welfare of its own people.

Hamas's War Crimes and the Truth Behind Genocide Claims

Hamas's actions—targeting civilians, using human shields, and deploying child soldiers—constituted war crimes under international law. Yet pro-Palestinian voices accused Israel of genocide. This claim was not only false but dangerous. Genocide is the deliberate annihilation of a people, and Israel's actions could not have been further from this definition. Its military operations targeted Hamas, not civilians, and it continued to allow aid into Gaza even while under attack.

The real tragedy lay with the Palestinian civilians who suffered under Hamas's rule. Instead of investing in their future, Hamas built a terror regime that used its own people as tools in its war against Israel. Civilians died not because of Israeli policies, but because of Hamas's deliberate choices.

While we're on the topic, let me also address the "ethnic cleansing" narrative that pro-Palestinians have been pushing for decades. This claim fell apart under even the slightest scrutiny. In 1948, the Palestinian population in the West Bank and Gaza was around 1.4 million. By 2024, it had skyrocketed to over 5.4 million—a massive fourfold increase. Ethnic cleansing, by definition, involves reducing or eliminating a population, not seeing it grow at one of the fastest rates in the world. How could anyone seriously talk about ethnic cleansing when the numbers told the exact opposite story? This claim was nothing more than a baseless propaganda tool that ignored reality.

Egypt's Closed Border: A Silent Reality in the Gaza Conflict

The war in Gaza sparked outrage and debate worldwide, with many pointing fingers at Israel while conveniently ignoring a glaring question: Why didn't Egypt, which shared a border with Gaza, step in to accept refugees or provide aid? Wars throughout history have inevitably led to refugees—millions fled Ukraine, Syria, Iraq, and Afghanistan during their respective conflicts—but Gaza remained a stark exception.

Egypt controls the Rafah border crossing, Gaza's only gateway to the outside world that wasn't managed by Israel. Yet instead of opening its doors to fleeing civilians, Egypt reinforced its border with additional troops and military barriers. The border remained tightly sealed, even as the international community accused Israel of failing to protect Gaza's civilians. Why did Egypt, an Arab nation with a shared cultural and historical connection to Palestinians, take such a hardline stance?

The answer lay in Egypt's deep-seated concerns about Hamas and the radical jihadist ideology it represented. Egypt viewed Hamas not just as a terrorist organization but as a destabilizing force capable of spreading extremism across its own borders. In 2013, Egypt's military ousted the Muslim Brotherhood from power—a group ideologically aligned with Hamas. Since then, Cairo had taken every precaution to prevent Hamas's influence from seeping into its territory.

Radical jihadists posed a serious threat to Egypt's stability. The Sinai Peninsula, which borders Gaza, had been a hotbed of extremist activity for years, with groups like ISIS targeting Egyptian security forces. Allowing an uncontrolled influx of refugees—among whom Hamas fighters and operatives could easily hide—would have been a security nightmare for Egypt. It wasn't just about humanitarian concerns—it was about protecting the nation from a potential wave of violence and chaos.

The world's silence on Egypt's role exposed a glaring double standard. Why was Israel expected to provide aid, power, and water to Gaza—even while Hamas launched rockets at its cities—while Egypt faced no such demands? Why was Israel criticized for defending its borders, but Egypt's border reinforcement was met with tacit acceptance?

Egypt's actions highlighted an uncomfortable truth: even neighboring Arab states recognized the dangers posed by Hamas. They understood that opening the Rafah crossing unconditionally would not just bring innocent refugees but also arms, fighters, and the ideology of radical jihadism that had already plagued the region.

The Unacknowledged Responsibility of Arab Nations

This situation underscored the broader failure of the Arab world to support Palestinians in any meaningful way. While leaders issued fiery statements condemning Israel, they offered little in terms of tangible aid or solutions. Refugee camps were a common sight in conflicts around the globe, yet none were established in Egypt across Gaza's southern border.

Instead, Palestinians were left to suffer under Hamas's rule, while the international narrative unfairly placed the entire burden on Israel.

If the international community had been serious about addressing the humanitarian crisis in Gaza, it would have held Egypt and other Arab nations accountable for their role. Why was the burden of caring for Gaza's civilians placed solely on Israel—a nation under attack—while Arab states refused to shoulder any responsibility?

Recognizing the True Villain

This war was never a fight against the Palestinian people; it was a fight against Hamas—a terrorist organization that thrived on death, chaos, and human suffering. Israel's right to defend itself was never up for debate. The world needed to understand that the root cause of the conflict was not Israel's response, but Hamas's unrelenting commitment to terror and its exploitation of civilians as shields.

Hamas brought devastation not only to Israeli towns but also to the very people it claimed to represent. It turned hospitals into command centers, schools into weapons depots, and neighborhoods into battlefields. The true path to peace lay in holding Hamas accountable—not just for the bloodshed it caused among Israelis, but for the misery it inflicted upon Palestinians. Only once the world recognized this reality could there be hope for a future where both peoples might finally live in peace.

Chapter 11

Is Anti-Israel Sentiment the New Face of Antisemitism?

The global response to the Israeli-Palestinian conflict has exposed some deeply troubling patterns. In recent years, and especially after the horrific October 7 attacks by Hamas, criticism of Israel has often crossed the line into outright antisemitism. Thousands of Israeli civilians were murdered in those attacks, but within hours, protests erupted around the world—not in solidarity with the victims, but against Israel. This kind of reaction raises a tough question: when does opposition to Israel become a cover for age-old antisemitism?

A Glaring Double Standard

Here's a hard truth to confront: why does Israel get so much attention compared to other conflicts? The numbers don't add up:

- Over half a million people died in the **Congo War**. Where were the protests?
- In **Syria**, Bashar al-Assad's regime killed more than half a million civilians, using barrel bombs and chemical weapons on his own people. Where were the university sit-ins? Where were the students storming buildings to demand action?
- In **Yemen**, **Iraq**, **Sudan**, and **Afghanistan**, hundreds of thousands have perished—but there's been no global outcry on the same scale.
- In **China**, over a million Uyghur Muslims have been detained in camps, subjected to indoctrination, forced labor, and cultural erasure. Where is the global outcry?
- Even the **2017 Battle of Mosul**, where 40,000 civilians died due to U.S., UK, and Jordanian actions, didn't generate worldwide protests.

The Battle of Mosul, much like the war in Gaza, involved urban combat against a terrorist organization entrenched within civilian areas. Both conflicts led to devastating civilian casualties as militaries faced the grim reality of fighting enemies who use human shields. Yet the reactions to these two wars couldn't be more different. Mosul's civilian death toll of **40,000** barely registered in global media, while Gaza dominates headlines, with narratives that disproportionately blame Israel for the consequences of Hamas's tactics. This stark disparity reveals a troubling bias against the Jewish state.

How is it possible that Assad's genocide, which included the use of sarin gas on children, didn't spark mass protests in the streets of Western cities or coordinated global outrage? Why didn't students occupy university buildings demanding accountability for Assad's atrocities? The silence is deafening and deeply revealing.

Dangerous Rhetoric: "From the River to the Sea"

One of the most popular chants at these protests is "From the river to the sea, Palestine will be free." At first glance, it might sound like a call for liberation, but let's unpack it. This phrase effectively demands the elimination of Israel. It's not about coexistence; it's about wiping out the only Jewish state and its seven million Jewish residents. That's not just political activism—it's antisemitism, plain and simple.

This chant has been echoed in rallies around the globe, often accompanied by imagery and rhetoric glorifying violence. After the October 7 attacks, some protesters even celebrated Hamas's brutality, waving flags and chanting slogans that effectively endorsed terrorism. Such open displays of hate reflect a chilling normalization of antisemitism in modern political movements.

Social Media: The Hate Machine

Social media platforms have become breeding grounds for misinformation and hate. False narratives about Israel spread rapidly, often using highly edited or out-of-context images and videos to vilify the Jewish state. For example:

- **Fake Atrocities:** Viral posts accused Israel of bombing a hospital in Gaza, killing 500 people. Within days, it was revealed that the explosion was caused by a failed rocket launched by Islamic Jihad, and that the number of casualties was far lower. Yet by then, the lie had gone viral, fueling protests and antisemitic attacks worldwide.
- **Distorted Humanitarian Claims:** Posts claiming Israel deliberately cut off Gaza's water and electricity were shared millions of times. In reality, Hamas damaged key infrastructure and hoarded resources, while Israel continued to provide humanitarian aid even during active conflict. The correction barely made a ripple.
- **Recycled Imagery:** Old photos and videos from unrelated wars— Syria, Iraq, even natural disasters—were rebranded as "evidence" of Israeli war crimes. One viral photo showing a soldier beating a child was actually taken during a protest in Chile. Another showed a Syrian bombing, labeled "Israeli airstrike on Gaza."
- **AI-Generated Propaganda:** The 2023–2024 war saw a surge of AI-generated "war photos" — hyper-realistic yet completely fake images showing children under rubble, burning hospitals, or mass graves. Many went viral before being debunked, some even featured in media outlets. These synthetic fakes exploit human empathy and make propaganda harder than ever to distinguish from reality.
- **Exploiting the Sick and Vulnerable:** Photos of children suffering from genetic disorders or cancer were circulated as images of "starving Gazans," and even appeared in traditional media without verification. These emotional manipulations are designed to demonize Israel and inflame outrage.
- **The "$7000" Lie:** Pro-Israel posts and videos are often met with comments like "$7000," implying that Israel pays influencers or citizens to post supportive content. This echoes classic antisemitic conspiracy theories about Jews "buying influence" or "controlling

the media." It's a modern mutation of age-old hate, now wrapped in the language of social media cynicism.

- **Blood Libel 2.0:** Memes and tweets claiming Israel "harvests organs" from Palestinians have gained traction on fringe networks and even mainstream platforms, reviving medieval antisemitic myths that once fueled pogroms.
- **Doctored "Celebrations":** Videos supposedly showing Israelis rejoicing at Palestinian suffering are often heavily edited or taken out of context. Meanwhile, footage of Hamas militants and crowds celebrating real massacres of civilians is conveniently ignored.
- **The "Disappearing Palestine" Maps:** These viral infographics— shared endlessly by celebrities and activists—falsely depict Israel as having "erased" Palestinian land. They omit the legal, historical, and political realities: the British Mandate divisions, rejected partition plans, and repeated refusals of peace offers. The maps may provoke emotion, but they erase truth.

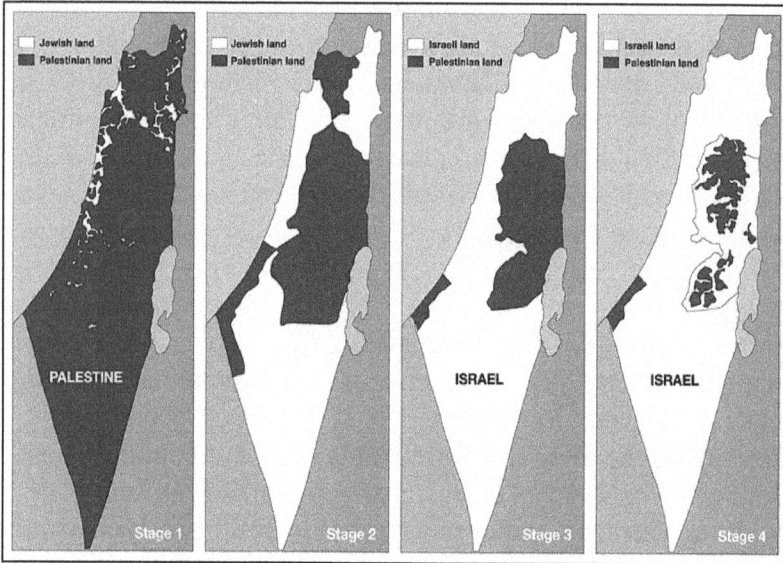

The "Disappearing Palestine Maps" misrepresent history by suggesting a sovereign Palestinian state once existed. The first map: British control, not Palestinian sovereignty. The second map: UN Partition Plan, rejected by Arab leaders. The third map: Jordanian and Egyptian control of the West Bank and Gaza from 1949 to 1967. The fourth map: Palestinian Authority-administered areas following the Oslo Accords. Source: Palestine Solidarity Campaign / Wikimedia Commons / CC BY 2.0

Algorithms play a significant role in amplifying this hate. Content that demonizes Israel gets more engagement, leading to a cycle where inflammatory posts are prioritized. This creates an echo chamber where lies and antisemitic tropes gain legitimacy. Meanwhile, voices countering these narratives are often drowned out or silenced entirely.

Social media also glorifies acts of terrorism. After the October 7 attacks, celebratory videos of Hamas fighters infiltrating Israeli territory went viral. Posts praising the paragliders used to carry out the massacre were widely shared, normalizing violence and erasing the humanity of the victims. This isn't just misinformation; it's propaganda designed to incite hate.

Academia: Fueling Bias and Antisemitism

What's even more shocking is how much of this bias comes from universities. Professors and student groups demonize Israel while turning a blind eye to atrocities committed by others. This selective outrage creates an environment where antisemitism thrives under the guise of social justice. Jewish students are left feeling unsafe and unwelcome, while administrators often look the other way.

After October 7, some academics went so far as to justify or even celebrate the attacks. Statements from prominent professors framed Hamas's actions as "resistance," ignoring the horrific reality of mass killings, kidnappings, and sexual violence.

Parallels to Nazi-Era Antisemitism

The parallels between today's anti-Israel sentiment and the antisemitism of Nazi Germany are chilling. During the 1930s and 1940s, Nazi-controlled media and academia were key instruments of dehumanization. Schools indoctrinated children with pseudoscientific race theories portraying Jews as parasites and corrupters of society. Universities lent these lies an air of intellectual legitimacy, publishing journals and hosting lectures that framed hatred as "scholarship." From classrooms to newspapers, propaganda saturated everyday life, normalizing antisemitism as patriotism.

Today's academia doesn't teach race theories, but the pattern is hauntingly familiar. Professors openly vilify Israel, describing it as a "settler-colonial" or "apartheid" state, while downplaying or excusing acts of terrorism. Student organizations distribute materials that echo classic antisemitic tropes — the greedy manipulator, the global conspirator — repackaged as "anti-Zionist" activism. Campus demonstrations feature chants like "Globalize the Intifada" and "From the River to the Sea," thinly veiled calls for Israel's destruction. The same institutions that once prided themselves on moral clarity now serve as incubators for hate wrapped in academic language.

Meanwhile, mainstream and social media amplify these narratives uncritically, presenting Israel as a singular embodiment of evil while ignoring far greater atrocities in countries like Syria, Iran, and China. This obsessive fixation — the idea that the world's only Jewish state is uniquely illegitimate — mirrors the scapegoating of Jews in the 1930s: a small minority blamed for the world's problems.

Just as Nazi propaganda once laid the groundwork for the Holocaust, today's rhetoric against Israel fuels real-world violence against Jews across the globe. Synagogues are vandalized, Jewish businesses targeted, and individuals harassed, assaulted, and even murdered — all incited by a relentless stream of hate flowing from universities, protests, and online platforms. The tools have changed, but the objective is the same: to isolate, delegitimize, and ultimately erase the Jewish presence from public life.

The Role of Qatar - the largest foreign donor to American universities

Qatar, a nation enriched by its vast natural gas reserves, has openly aligned itself with Hamas and the Muslim Brotherhood, organizations infamous for their anti-Israel and anti-Semitic agendas. Hamas has received both financial support and political backing from Qatar, which has also hosted its leaders in Doha. The Muslim Brotherhood, a similarly controversial organization with a history of promoting radical ideologies, has benefited from Qatar's largesse as well. This alignment raises serious questions about Qatar's broader agenda and its attempts to shape narratives far beyond its borders.

One area where Qatar's influence has been particularly significant is U.S. academia. Over two decades, Qatar has become the largest foreign donor to American universities, contributing an astounding $4.7 billion from 2001 to 2021. Institutions such as Cornell University, which received $1.95 billion, and Georgetown University, with over $210 million in funding, have been key beneficiaries of this financial relationship. While these contributions are often framed as investments in education, many worry that they come with strings attached. Is it possible that Qatar's financial support may be used to promote pro-Hamas and anti-Israel sentiments on campuses, subtly shaping academic programs and creating an environment hostile to Jewish students and Israel?

These concerns demand greater scrutiny. Universities are meant to be safe spaces for open inquiry and unbiased education, not platforms for foreign governments to push their political agendas. Accepting large sums from a nation that supports terrorism and groups with anti-Israel ideologies risks undermining the values these institutions are supposed to uphold.

Chapter 12

The Genetic Case

Pro-Palestinians often claim that Israeli Jews are Europeans. I'm about to expose a surprising fact - **modern-day Palestinians have more European DNA than most Israeli Jews!**

The myth that Israeli Jews are primarily of European descent is debunked by modern genetic research. The 2020 *Cell* study and others show that while Ashkenazi Jews carry some European DNA from centuries in the diaspora, Mizrahi Jews—nearly half of Israel's Jewish population—retain the strongest genetic continuity with ancient Canaanites and the Levant. By contrast, modern Palestinians carry European and Central Asian admixture at levels comparable to Ashkenazi Jews, introduced largely through Arab and Ottoman-era migrations.

This discovery didn't come out of nowhere. Earlier genetic studies had already revealed the same pattern. In 2010, two landmark papers—one published in *Nature* (Behar et al.) and another in *The American Journal of Human Genetics* (Atzmon et al.)—compared Jewish and non-Jewish populations across the globe. Both found that **Ashkenazi, Sephardi, and Mizrahi Jews share a common Middle-Eastern genetic core**, distinct from their European or North-African host populations.

A few years later, *Haber et al.* (*PLoS Genetics*, 2013) mapped how migrations from Arabia and nearby regions shaped local DNA, showing that Jewish groups cluster genetically with other Levantine peoples rather than with newcomers from the Arabian Peninsula. Then *Waldman et al.* (*Cell*, 2022) analyzed medieval Jewish remains from Germany and found that 14th-century Ashkenazim already carried the same Middle-Eastern genetic signature seen today, proving these roots long predate the modern era. Together, these studies paved the way for

167

the landmark *Cell* (2020) paper — the first to compare modern populations with DNA taken directly from Canaanite-era skeletons.

2020 *Cell* Study

Cell is one of the world's most respected scientific journals, known for publishing groundbreaking research in genetics and molecular biology.

In 2020, it published *The Genetic History of the Southern Levant* — one of the most comprehensive DNA studies ever done on the region. Researchers extracted DNA from **Bronze-Age human remains in Sidon (modern Lebanon)** to create a genetic benchmark for the ancient Canaanites. They then compared these ancient genomes with those of modern populations — including **Palestinians, Lebanese, Syrians, and various Jewish groups** — to trace genetic continuity and admixture across millennia.

Using next-generation sequencing and an interdisciplinary approach that combined genetics with archaeology and history, the study provided clear evidence of genetic continuity between ancient Canaanites and modern Jewish populations, especially Mizrahi and Sephardi Jews. Its rigorous methodology and peer-reviewed publication in *Cell* make it one of the most credible scientific sources on the subject.

Key strengths of the study include:

- **Advanced Techniques:** The use of next-generation sequencing ensured high accuracy and detail in genetic analysis.
- **Wide Sampling:** Ancient DNA from Canaanite-era remains was compared with modern DNA from Palestinians, Lebanese, Syrians, and various Jewish populations.
- **Peer Review:** Published in a leading scientific journal, the study underwent rigorous peer review, making it a reliable source for understanding genetic links in the Levant.

Historical Events That Shaped Jewish and Palestinian DNA

The DNA of both Jews and Palestinians reflects the turbulent history of the Levant — a region repeatedly reshaped by **invasions, exiles, and mass migrations** over thousands of years.

- **Roman Occupation and Jewish Exile (70–136 CE):** After the destruction of the Second Temple and the Bar Kokhba revolt, the Romans expelled large segments of the Jewish population from Judea. This forced diaspora scattered Jews across the Middle East, North Africa, and Europe, where gradual intermarriage introduced new genetic layers. As a result, modern Jewish groups — especially Ashkenazim — retain roughly **50–60 % Levantine ancestry**, with the rest reflecting European and regional admixture acquired during centuries of exile.

- **Crusader Massacres and Rule (1099–1187 CE):** When Crusader forces captured Jerusalem in 1099, they massacred much of the city's Jewish and Muslim population. The establishment of European enclaves and settlements during the Crusader Kingdom further altered the local gene pool. This upheaval greatly reduced the continuous Jewish presence in the region, contributing to the lower genetic continuity among later-returning Jewish populations.

- **Arab and Ottoman Conquests (7th–19th centuries CE):** The Arab conquest of the 7th century brought substantial Arabian-Peninsula genetic input into the Levant, particularly among populations that later identified as Palestinian and Jordanian. Under Ottoman rule, additional migrations from the Balkans, Anatolia, and Central Asia introduced new European and Central-Asian elements — reflected today in the 15–25% non-Levantine ancestry observed among Palestinians.

These historical disruptions explain why Jewish DNA shows partial dilution from centuries of diaspora, while Palestinian DNA reflects multiple external migrations layered onto a shared ancient Levantine base. The genetic record, in other words, mirrors the historical record — a land constantly conquered, resettled, and yet still carrying echoes of its ancient inhabitants.

Palestinian Genetic Composition

Modern Palestinians' DNA reflects the region's turbulent history of migrations and conquests. While Palestinians do share ancestry with ancient Canaanites, their genetic profile includes significant contributions from later populations:

- **Levantine Ancestry:** Approximately **45-50%** of Palestinian DNA is linked to ancient Canaanites and other Bronze Age Levantine populations.

- **Arabian Influence:** Around **30%** of Palestinian DNA reflects Arabian ancestry introduced during the Islamic conquests in the 7th century CE.

- **Balkan, European, and Central Asian Contributions:** Around **15-20%** of Palestinian DNA is linked to populations from the Balkans, Europe, and Central Asia. These contributions were introduced primarily during the Ottoman Empire (1517–1917) through administrative relocations, military campaigns, and intermarriage.

- **North African**: Around **5-10%** of Palestinian DNA reflects North African ancestry

This diverse genetic profile highlights the significant impact of historical migrations and conquests on the Palestinian population, diluting their direct genetic ties to ancient Levantine populations.

Mizrahi Jews (Half of Israel's Jewish population)

In contrast, Mizrahi Jews, who have historically resided in the Middle East and North Africa, retain a genetic profile with **stronger ties to the ancient Levant**:

- **Levantine Ancestry:** The 2020 *Cell* study shows that Mizrahi Jews have **65-80% of their DNA** linked to ancient Canaanites and other Bronze Age Levantine populations. This percentage reflects a direct and continuous presence in or near the region for millennia.

- **Minimal Admixture:** Mizrahi Jews experienced less genetic admixture compared to other Jewish groups in the diaspora, such as Ashkenazi and Sephardi Jews. This limited external influence preserved their strong genetic continuity with the Levant.

- **Mesopotamian and Persian Influences:** The remaining DNA of Mizrahi Jews primarily reflects historical interactions within the broader Middle East, including Mesopotamian/Persian populations, rather than contributions from European or Central Asian groups.

Ashkenazi (European) Jews (25% of Israel's population)

Ashkenazi (European) Jews also share ancestry with ancient Canaanites but exhibit a more complex genetic profile due to significant admixture during centuries of diaspora:

- **Levantine Ancestry:** Approximately **45-60%** of Ashkenazi Jewish DNA is linked to ancient Canaanites and Levantine populations.

- **European Admixture: 25-35%** European ancestry introduced during their long residence in Europe.

- **15-25% Middle Eastern and Other:** Includes Mesopotamian, Persian, Anatolian, and North African contributions, as well as shared Jewish-specific markers.

- **Jewish Genetic Cohesion:** Despite admixture, Ashkenazi Jews retain a genetic core that ties them to other Jewish populations and the Levant, underscoring their shared origins.

Group	Levantine/ Canaanite Ancestry	Arabian Influence	Middle Eastern / North African	Balkan / European / Caucasus Influence
Palestinians	40-50%	~30%	15-20%	5–10%
Mizrahi Jews	~65-80%	<10%	~15-25%	Minimal
Sephardi Jews	55–70%	Minimal	20–30%	10–20%
Ashkenazi Jews	~45-60%	Minimal	15–25%	25-35%

Conclusion: A Stronger Genetic Connection

Modern genomic research reveals that **Mizrahi Jews**, who make up nearly 50% of Israel's Jewish population, preserve the most direct genetic continuity with the ancient peoples of the Southern Levant, the region historically associated with Canaanite and early Israelite civilizations. This finding emerges consistently across multiple large-scale studies and ancient-DNA comparisons.

1. **Higher Canaanite Ancestry**: Genome-wide analyses and ancient-DNA comparisons show that Mizrahi Jews retain the highest proportion of ancestry derived from Bronze- and Iron-Age Levantine populations—the genetic profile that defines the ancient Canaanites (*Agranat-Tamir et al., Cell 2020*). Having remained within or near the region for millennia, they show minimal dilution of this ancestral component.

2. **Lower External Influence**: While Palestinians and Jordanians exhibit significant Arabian-Peninsula and East-African admixture introduced during the Islamic expansions, Mizrahi Jews show negligible Arabian or European input. Their genetic signatures align more closely with ancient Near-Eastern and early Israelite lineages than with surrounding host populations.

3. **Preservation of Levantine Identity**: Despite centuries of dispersion, Jewish populations form a tight genetic cluster rooted in the Levant (*Behar et al., Nature 2010; Atzmon et al., AJHG 2010*). The genomes of Mizrahi Jews, in particular, reflect a direct line of continuity from ancient Levantine ancestors, highlighting an enduring connection to the historical homeland.

Collectively, these findings confirm that Mizrahi Jews—who comprise nearly half of Israel's Jewish population—are genetically closer to ancient Canaanite and Israelite populations than any other modern group. Ashkenazi and Sephardi Jews share this Levantine core but acquired additional European or North-African admixture during the diaspora. In contrast, modern Palestinians and Jordanians, though retaining part of the same ancestral base, exhibit heavier Arabian-Peninsula admixture, reflecting later demographic shifts.

In short, modern genetics affirms that the Jewish people—especially their Mizrahi branch—are not recent arrivals to the Levant but direct descendants of its ancient inhabitants, maintaining stronger genetic continuity with the Canaanite–Israelite population than any other extant community.

Chapter 13

Israel - A Vibrant, Successful Democracy

The outrageous pro-Palestinian claim that Israel is a racist, apartheid state is not just baseless—it's a deliberate distortion of reality aimed at delegitimizing the world's only Jewish state. Israel is a thriving democracy in the Middle East, a region dominated by authoritarian regimes, and it stands out as a beacon of freedom, equality, and opportunity for all its citizens, regardless of ethnicity or religion.

Israel's Commitment to Peace

Israel's history and actions reveal a profound commitment to peace and coexistence, even in the face of relentless hostility. Over the decades, Israel has pursued and achieved peace agreements with its neighbors, often making significant concessions to foster stability in the region. The peace treaty with Egypt in 1979, which included the complete withdrawal from the Sinai Peninsula—**an area three times the size of Israel**—demonstrated Israel's willingness to trade land for peace. Similarly, the 1994 treaty with Jordan resolved longstanding disputes, creating a lasting partnership that has endured despite regional challenges. More recently, the Abraham Accords normalized relations with several Arab states, including the UAE, Bahrain, Sudan, and Morocco, proving that dialogue and cooperation are possible in the region.

Israel's pursuit of peace is not just a political strategy; it is a reflection of its core values. This commitment is perhaps best expressed by Golda Meir, who said, *"Peace will come when the Arabs love their children more than they hate us."* Her words poignantly capture the tragedy of a conflict driven by hatred and rejection of Israel's existence. Extremist groups like Hamas continue to prioritize violence and refuse to recognize Israel's right to exist, despite the toll this takes on their own people. Yet Israel remains steadfast, balancing the need to protect its citizens with the hope of one day achieving true peace.

A Society of Equality and Opportunity in Israel

Israeli Arabs, who make up about 21% of the population, enjoy full citizenship rights. They vote, serve in the Knesset (parliament), and hold key positions across various sectors. Where else in the Middle East can you find Arab lawmakers shaping national policy in a parliament alongside Jewish colleagues? For example, Arab Justice Salim Joubran served as a Supreme Court justice and was part of the panel that convicted a Jewish former Prime Minister, Ehud Olmert. Arabs also serve as diplomats, university professors, CEOs, and leaders in public institutions—a level of representation unimaginable in most neighboring countries.

Israel's defense forces, often targeted by critics, include Druze, Bedouin, Christians, and even Arab Muslim soldiers who voluntarily enlist and serve with distinction. These individuals are not token participants; they take on leadership roles and fight shoulder to shoulder with Jewish soldiers to protect the freedoms that all Israeli citizens enjoy. Arab, Druze and Bedouin soldiers actively defend Israel from Hamas's relentless terror campaigns, further debunking the racist accusations.

Let's talk about the quality of life for Arabs in Israel. In a region where basic human rights are often trampled, Israel ensures freedom of speech, religion, and assembly for all its citizens. Arab Israelis enjoy access to some of the best healthcare, education, and employment opportunities in the Middle East. They attend Israeli universities, often with government scholarships, and play an integral role in the country's medical system as doctors, nurses, and researchers. These opportunities are a far cry from the oppression and lack of basic freedoms faced by Arabs in many surrounding countries.

And what about LGBTQ+ rights? Israel is the only country in the region where LGBTQ+ individuals—including Arabs—can live openly without fear of persecution. While in much of the Arab world LGBTQ+ people face imprisonment or even death, Israel celebrates diversity. Tel Aviv

Pride is one of the largest events of its kind globally, and LGBTQ+ rights are enshrined in the country's laws. This stark contrast highlights Israel's commitment to individual freedoms and human dignity.

The so-called "apartheid wall" is another favorite accusation of Israel's detractors. Let's set the record straight: this barrier is not about segregation; it's about survival. Built during the Second Intifada, it was a necessary response to waves of suicide bombings and terrorist attacks that killed hundreds of innocent civilians. The barrier, which runs between Israel and the West Bank—territory controlled by the Palestinian Authority—has saved countless lives by dramatically reducing these attacks. Calling it an "apartheid wall" is a grotesque misrepresentation of a measure designed to protect people, not to divide them.

If we're talking about apartheid, it's worth examining the Palestinian territories. Jews are entirely barred from living in Gaza, where any who enter will probably get lynched within minutes. In the West Bank, the Palestinian Authority openly demands the removal of Jewish settlements and denies Jews access to religious sites like the Tomb of the Patriarchs in Hebron and Joseph's Tomb in Nablus. This systematic exclusion and outright hostility toward Jewish presence represent a true apartheid-like system, starkly contrasting with Israel, where Arabs enjoy full civil rights, vote in elections, and participate at every level of society.

Israel's multicultural fabric is unparalleled in the region. Jews from Ethiopia, India, Europe, the Middle East, and beyond have found a home in Israel. This diversity extends to its Arab citizens, who speak their language freely, see Arabic on street signs and official documents, and operate independent media outlets. Contrast this with the reality in Gaza and the West Bank, where free speech is suppressed, and dissent is met with brutal force by Hamas and the Palestinian Authority.

The truth is that the Israeli-Palestinian conflict is not about race, rights or dignity, but about the refusal of extremist groups like Hamas to accept the existence of a Jewish state. Hamas's charter openly calls for Israel's destruction. Israel's actions, including its military responses, are about defending its citizens from terrorism, not oppressing another people.

Israel is not just a democracy—it's a thriving, inclusive society that offers freedoms and opportunities unmatched anywhere else in the region. The baseless accusations of apartheid and racism are not just lies; they're an insult to the millions of Israelis, both Jews and Arabs, who live and work together to build a better future. It's time to reject these falsehoods and recognize Israel for what it truly is: a beacon of hope and freedom in an often-hostile region.

Israel's Economic Success

Israel's transformation into an economic powerhouse is a remarkable story of resilience and innovation. With a GDP per capita exceeding $50,000, Israel outpaces not only its Middle Eastern neighbors like Egypt, Jordan, Lebanon, and Syria, where GDP per capita often remains below $5,000, but also several prominent European nations, including the United Kingdom, Italy and Spain. This extraordinary achievement underscores the power of strategic investment in education, technology, and infrastructure, benefiting all citizens of Israel, including Jews, Arabs, Druze, and Bedouins.

In stark contrast to its neighbors, Israel has embraced a knowledge-based economy built on innovation. Dubbed the "Startup Nation," it leads globally in fields like cybersecurity, biotechnology, and artificial intelligence. These advancements attract significant foreign investment, create high-paying jobs, and drive sustained growth. Unlike many Arab countries in the region, whose economies rely heavily on natural resources or low-value exports, Israel's focus on high-tech industries and diversification has enabled it to flourish.

This economic prosperity has brought tangible benefits to Arab Israelis as well. Targeted programs have increased their participation in high-tech sectors, improved education in Arab-majority towns, and provided critical agricultural innovations, such as drip irrigation and desalination technologies, to rural communities. By bridging historical economic gaps, these efforts empower minority groups and foster a more inclusive society.

The disparity between Israel and its Arab neighbors highlights the impact of strategic policies. While Jordan and Egypt face challenges like resource scarcity and underinvestment in education, Israel's commitment to innovation has propelled it into global prominence. Furthermore, economic success fosters coexistence within Israel, as shared opportunities in business, healthcare, and public services create connections across diverse communities.

Israeli Inventions and Contributions Across Industries

Technology and Cybersecurity

1. **Mobileye:** A global leader in autonomous driving and advanced driver-assistance systems, acquired by Intel for $15 billion.
2. **Waze:** A navigation app revolutionizing real-time driving and navigation, acquired by Google.
3. **Check Point Software Technologies:** A pioneer in cybersecurity solutions used by businesses and governments worldwide.
4. **ICQ:** One of the first instant messaging platforms, laying the groundwork for modern communication tools.
5. **CyberArk** – Protects critical digital infrastructure by managing privileged access, preventing data breaches across hospitals, banks, and governments.
6. **OrCam** – AI-powered wearable technology that enables the visually impaired to read, recognize faces, and navigate the world independently.

7. **Mellanox Technologies** – Provides the high-speed networking backbone for global AI, cloud computing, and scientific supercomputers.

Healthcare and Medicine

1. **PillCam:** A tiny, ingestible camera that revolutionized gastrointestinal diagnostics, enabling non-invasive internal imaging.
2. **Teva Pharmaceuticals:** A world leader in generic drugs, providing affordable healthcare solutions globally.
3. **ReWalk:** A wearable exoskeleton that helps paraplegics walk again, transforming lives for people with spinal cord injuries.
4. **BrainsWay** – Developed Deep Transcranial Magnetic Stimulation (TMS) to treat depression and OCD without drugs or invasive procedures.
5. **IceCure Medical** – Created cryoablation technology that freezes and destroys tumors without surgery, reducing recovery time and risk.
6. **Alpha Tau Medical (Alpha DaRT)** – Introduced a groundbreaking cancer therapy using localized alpha radiation to eradicate solid tumors.
7. **Itamar Medical (WatchPAT)** – A simple, at-home sleep apnea diagnostic device improving global access to sleep disorder treatment.
8. **Nano-Retina** – Developing a bionic retina implant that could restore sight to the blind.

Agriculture and Water Management

1. **Drip Irrigation:** Developed by Netafim, this innovation revolutionized agriculture by enabling efficient water use and boosting crop yields worldwide.
2. **Watergen:** A device that extracts potable water from the air, solving water scarcity issues in remote and arid regions.

3. **Desalination Plants:** Israel leads the world in desalination, providing nearly 80% of its drinking water through cutting-edge facilities.

4. **Hybrid Crops:** Israeli scientists developed drought-resistant crops, ensuring agricultural sustainability in challenging climates.

5. **BioBee Biological Systems** – Exports beneficial insects for natural pest control, reducing pesticide use and protecting pollinators.

6. **Tal-Ya Water Technologies** – Created reusable dew-collection trays that reduce water loss and improve yields in dry regions.

7. **AKOL** – Provides farmers with AI-based crop monitoring and data systems that boost efficiency and reduce waste.

Energy and Sustainability

1. **SolarEdge:** A global leader in solar energy optimization, helping to make renewable energy more efficient and accessible.

2. **Renewable Gas Technology:** Israeli companies have pioneered systems to convert organic waste into clean, renewable energy.

3. **StoreDot** – Developed ultra-fast-charging EV batteries, capable of reaching full charge in minutes, helping accelerate clean transportation.

4. **HomeBiogas** – Converts household organic waste into clean cooking gas and liquid fertilizer, improving energy independence and sanitation.

5. **Brenmiller Energy** – Developed thermal energy storage systems that make renewable power reliable and grid-stable.

Defense and Security

1. **Iron Dome:** A missile defense system that protects civilians and is recognized as one of the most effective in the world.
2. **Rafael Advanced Defense Systems:** Innovators in cutting-edge military and defense technologies that are also adapted for civilian use.
3. **Trophy Active Protection System** – Protects armored vehicles by intercepting incoming missiles; now used by the U.S. Army.
4. **David's Sling** – Intercepts medium-range missiles, forming part of Israel's multilayered missile defense network.
5. **Elbit Systems** – Developer of UAVs, helmet-mounted displays for pilots, and border-monitoring systems used globally for defense and rescue.

Other Industries and Everyday Innovations

1. **USB Flash Drive:** Invented by Israeli engineers, revolutionizing portable data storage.
2. **Epilator:** An innovative hair removal device developed in Israel, widely used across the globe.
3. **Cherry Tomatoes:** Perfected by Israeli agricultural scientists to enhance shelf life and flavor, they are now a global staple.
4. **Cow Monitoring Systems:** Israeli farmers created systems to monitor livestock health and milk production, boosting efficiency in dairy farming.
5. **Online Banking Security Systems:** Innovations in digital financial security used worldwide originated in Israel.
6. **BabySense** – A non-contact infant breathing monitor that has helped prevent countless cases of sudden infant death syndrome (SIDS).
7. **Lightricks** – Creator of Facetune and other creative apps that empower millions to express themselves visually.

A Model for the Region

Israel's story is more than a national success—it's a blueprint for what the Middle East could become. In less than a century, Israel transformed from a vulnerable new state into a thriving democracy and global innovation hub. Its achievements prove that progress in the region does not depend on oil or autocracy, but on education, entrepreneurship, and the rule of law.

Despite constant security threats, Israel has upheld free elections, an independent judiciary, and equal rights for all citizens, including Arabs, Druze, and Christians. This pluralistic democracy—where diversity coexists with freedom—stands in stark contrast to the authoritarianism that dominates much of the region.

Economically, Israel turned scarcity into strength. By investing in human talent and education, it became a global leader in technology, agriculture, water management, medicine, and renewable energy — fields that improve lives far beyond its borders. Nations worldwide now rely on Israeli know-how to fight hunger, disease, and climate challenges.

Through peace treaties with Egypt, Jordan, and the Abraham Accords, Israel also demonstrated that cooperation and coexistence are not utopian ideals—they are achievable realities.

Israel's example shows that prosperity, freedom, and stability can take root even in the Middle East's most difficult environment. It remains not just a success story, but a model for the region's future.

Bibliography

Chapter 1: The Ottoman Occupation (1516-1917)

1. "1905 Ottoman Census of Jerusalem." Ottoman Archives, Istanbul.
2. "1922 British Census of Palestine." British Colonial Office Records, The National Archives, London.
3. Cuinet, Vital. *La Syrie: Précis géographique, statistique, et archéologique.* Paris: Ernest Leroux, 1896.
4. Murray, John. *Handbook for Travellers in Syria and Palestine.* London: J. Murray, 1866.
5. Thomson, William McClure. *The Land and the Book: Biblical Illustrations Drawn from the Manners and Customs, the Scenes and Scenery of the Holy Land.* New York: Harper & Brothers, 1859.
6. Twain, Mark. *The Innocents Abroad.* Hartford: American Publishing Company, 1869.
7. Oliphant, Laurence. *Haifa, or Life in Modern Palestine.* London: Blackwood, 1887.
8. Lamartine, Alphonse de. *Voyage en Orient.* Paris: Editions d'Aujourd'hui, 1835.
9. Guerin, Victor. *Description géographique, historique et archéologique de la Palestine.* Paris: Imprimerie impériale, 1850.
10. Robinson, Edward. *Biblical Researches in Palestine, Mount Sinai, and Arabia Petraea.* Boston: Crocker and Brewster, 1841.
11. Keith, Alexander. *The Land of Israel: According to the Covenant with Abraham, with Isaac, and with Jacob.* Edinburgh: William Whyte, 1843.
12. McCarthy, Justin. *The Population of Palestine: Population History and Statistics of the Late Ottoman Period and the Mandate.* New York: Columbia University Press, 1990.
13. Karpat, Kemal H. *Ottoman Population, 1830-1914: Demographic and Social Characteristics.* Madison: University of Wisconsin Press, 1985.
14. Scholch, Alexander. "The Demographic Development of Palestine, 1850-1882." *International Journal of Middle East Studies,* vol. 17, no. 4, 1985, pp. 485–505.
15. Jewish National Fund (JNF). *Land Redemption Reports* (1858–1948). Internal Archives, Jerusalem.
16. Finn, James. *Byeways in Palestine.* London: James Nisbet and Co., 1868.
17. Pococke, Richard. *A Description of the East and Some Other Countries.* London: W. Bowyer, 1745.
18. Stephens, John Lloyd. *Incidents of Travel in Egypt, Arabia Petraea, and the Holy Land.* New York: Harper & Brothers, 1837.
19. Volney, Constantin-François. *Travels Through Syria and Egypt in the Years 1783, 1784, and 1785.* London: G.G.J. and J. Robinson, 1788.

20. Niebuhr, Carsten. *Reisebeschreibung nach Arabien und andern umliegenden Ländern.* Copenhagen: Nicolaus Möller, 1774.

21. Famin, César. *Jerusalem and Its Environs: Their History and Antiquities.* Paris: 1853.

22. British Consulate Reports, Jerusalem (1834–1917). British Foreign Office Archives, London.

23. Herzl, Theodor. *The Jewish State.* Leipzig & Vienna: M. Breitenstein's Verlags-Buchhandlung, 1896.

24. Sachar, Howard M. *A History of Israel from the Rise of Zionism to Our Time.* New York: Alfred A. Knopf, 2007.

25. Asbridge, Thomas. *The Crusades: The Authoritative History of the War for the Holy Land.* New York: HarperCollins, 2010.

26. Fulcher of Chartres. *A History of the Expedition to Jerusalem, 1095-1127.* Edited and translated by Martha Evelyn McGinty, 1969.

27. Goren, Haim. *Dead Sea Level: Science, Exploration and Imperial Interests in the Holy Land.* London: I.B. Tauris, 2011.

28. Shaare Zedek Hospital Archives. *Founding and Mission Records* (1902–1922). Internal Records, Jerusalem.

29. Ottoman Land Code of 1858. Official Documents from Ottoman Legal Reforms, Istanbul Archives.

30. Karsh, Efraim. *Palestine Betrayed.* New Haven: Yale University Press, 2010.

31. Segev, Tom. *One Palestine, Complete: Jews and Arabs Under the British Mandate.* New York: Metropolitan Books, 2000.

32. Shapira, Anita. *Land and Power: The Zionist Resort to Force, 1881-1948.* Stanford: Stanford University Press, 1992.

33. Cohen, Hillel. *Army of Shadows: Palestinian Collaboration with Zionism, 1917-1948.* Berkeley: University of California Press, 2008.

34. Lewis, Bernard. *The Middle East: A Brief History of the Last 2,000 Years.* New York: Scribner, 1995.

35. Porath, Yehoshua. *The Emergence of the Palestinian-Arab National Movement, 1918-1929.* London: Cass, 1974.

Chapter 2: The British Rule (1917-1948)

1. Sykes, Mark, and François Georges-Picot. *Sykes-Picot Agreement: Official Documents and Correspondence, 1916.* British Foreign Office Archives, London.

2. *League of Nations Mandate for Palestine,* July 24, 1922. League of Nations Archives, Geneva.

3. "British Census of Palestine, 1922." British Colonial Office Records, The National Archives, London.

4. "British Census of Palestine, 1931." British Colonial Office Records, The National Archives, London.

5. Cuinet, Vital. *La Syrie: Précis géographique, statistique, et archéologique.* Paris: Ernest Leroux, 1896.

6. McCarthy, Justin. *The Population of Palestine: Population History and Statistics of the Late Ottoman Period and the Mandate.* New York: Columbia University Press, 1990.

7. Karpat, Kemal H. *Ottoman Population, 1830-1914: Demographic and Social Characteristics.* Madison: University of Wisconsin Press, 1985.

8. Scholch, Alexander. "The Demographic Development of Palestine, 1850-1882." *International Journal of Middle East Studies*, vol. 17, no. 4, 1985, pp. 485–505.

9. Wasserstein, Bernard. *The British in Palestine: The Mandatory Government and the Arab-Jewish Conflict, 1917-1929.* Oxford: Basil Blackwell, 1991.

10. Gilbar, Gad G. *Population Dilemmas in the Middle East: Population History and Social Policy.* London: Frank Cass, 1997.

11. Segev, Tom. *One Palestine, Complete: Jews and Arabs Under the British Mandate.* New York: Metropolitan Books, 2000.

12. Porath, Yehoshua. *The Emergence of the Palestinian-Arab National Movement, 1918-1929.* London: Cass, 1974.

13. Arieh L. Avneri. *The Claim of Dispossession: Jewish Land-Settlement and the Arabs 1878–1948.* Tel Aviv: Hakibbutz Hameuchad Publishing House, 1984.

14. Herzl, Theodor. *The Jewish State.* Leipzig & Vienna: M. Breitenstein's Verlags-Buchhandlung, 1896.

15. Lewis, Bernard. *The Middle East: A Brief History of the Last 2,000 Years.* New York: Scribner, 1995.

16. Sachar, Howard M. *A History of Israel from the Rise of Zionism to Our Time.* New York: Alfred A. Knopf, 2007.

17. Oliphant, Laurence. *Haifa, or Life in Modern Palestine.* London: Blackwood, 1887.

18. Twain, Mark. *The Innocents Abroad.* Hartford: American Publishing Company, 1869.

19. Keith, Alexander. *The Land of Israel: According to the Covenant with Abraham, with Isaac, and with Jacob.* Edinburgh: William Whyte, 1843.

20. Robinson, Edward. *Biblical Researches in Palestine, Mount Sinai, and Arabia Petraea.* Boston: Crocker and Brewster, 1841.

21. Jack1956. "Ancient Jewish Coins Discovered at Masada." *Wikimedia Commons*, CC BY 3.0.

22. *Coins of the Anglo-Palestine Bank.* Internal Archival Records, Tel Aviv.

23. Finn, James. *Byeways in Palestine.* London: James Nisbet and Co., 1868.

24. Avineri, Shlomo. *The Making of Modern Zionism: The Intellectual Origins of the Jewish State.* New York: Basic Books, 1981.

25. Tobler, Titus. *Topography of Jerusalem.* Berlin: Verlag von Dietrich Reimer, 1853.

26. Lamartine, Alphonse de. *Voyage en Orient.* Paris: Editions d'Aujourd'hui, 1835.

27. Goren, Haim. *Dead Sea Level: Science, Exploration and Imperial Interests in the Holy Land.* London: I.B. Tauris, 2011.

28. Famin, César. *Jerusalem and Its Environs: Their History and Antiquities*. Paris: 1853.
29. *Palestine Electric Corporation Reports*. Internal Records, Haifa, 1923.
30. British Colonial Office. *Palestine: Annual Report of the British High Commissioner, 1920-1948*. The National Archives, London.
31. Ottolenghi, Emanuele. *Under the Shadow of the British Mandate: Palestine's Jewish National Institutions, 1920-1948*. Jerusalem: Yad Vashem, 2003.
32. Eshel, Hanan. *Masada: From Jewish Revolt to Modern National Icon*. Jerusalem: Israel Exploration Society, 2004.
33. Gilbert, Martin. *Israel: A History*. New York: HarperCollins, 1998.
34. Bar-Zohar, Michael. *Ben-Gurion: The Armed Prophet*. London: Weidenfeld and Nicolson, 1967.

Chapter 4: Jerusalem: Myths, Claims, and Realities

1. The Quran. Surah Al-Isra (17:1).
2. Grabar, Oleg. *The Shape of the Holy: Early Islamic Jerusalem*. Princeton: Princeton University Press, 1996.
3. Robinson, Edward. *Biblical Researches in Palestine, Mount Sinai, and Arabia Petraea*. Boston: Crocker and Brewster, 1841.
4. Mazar, Eilat. *The Palace of King David: Excavations at the Summit of the City of David Jerusalem 2005-2008*. Jerusalem: Shoham Academic Research and Publication, 2009.
5. Avigad, Nahman. *Discovering Jerusalem*. Nashville: Thomas Nelson, 1983.
6. Netanyahu, Benjamin. *A Durable Peace: Israel and Its Place Among the Nations*. New York: Warner Books, 2000.
7. Lewis, Bernard. *The Jews of Islam*. Princeton: Princeton University Press, 1984.
8. Hawting, Gerald R. *The First Dynasty of Islam: The Umayyad Caliphate AD 661-750*. London: Routledge, 2000.
9. Karsh, Efraim. *Islamic Imperialism: A History*. New Haven: Yale University Press, 2006.
10. The Arch of Titus. Steerpike, Wikimedia Commons, CC BY 3.0.
11. U.S. Department of State. "Announcement of U.S. Embassy Relocation to Jerusalem." December 6, 2017.
12. Gilbert, Martin. *Jerusalem: Rebirth of a City*. London: Weidenfeld and Nicolson, 1985.

Chapter 5: The Jewish Resistance

1. Aaronsohn, Sarah. *Letters and Writings of Sarah Aaronsohn*. Haifa University Press, 1968.
2. Bar-Zohar, Michael. *The Armed Resistance*. Yedioth Ahronoth, 1966.

3. Begin, Menachem. *The Revolt: Story of the Irgun.* Steimatzky, 1951.
4. Clarke, Thurston. *By Blood and Fire: The Attack on the King David Hotel.* Putnam, 1981.
5. Gilbert, Martin. *The Jews in the Twentieth Century: An Illustrated History.* Schocken, 2001.
6. Kagan, Erich. *The Zion Mule Corps and the Jewish Legion: Historical Contributions.* Cambridge Judaic Press, 1983.
7. Sachar, Howard M. *A History of Israel: From the Rise of Zionism to Our Time.* Knopf, 2007.
8. Schechtman, Joseph B. *The History of Jewish Resistance.* Philosophical Library, 1948.
9. Segev, Tom. *One Palestine, Complete: Jews and Arabs under the British Mandate.* Metropolitan Books, 2001.
10. Wistrich, Robert S. *The Essential Herzl: The Complete Theodor Herzl Collection.* Herzl Press, 1997.
11. Yadin, Yigael. *The Story of Masada.* Random House, 1966.
12. Central Zionist Archives, Jerusalem. Archival collections.

Chapter 6: The Establishment of Israel

1. Gilbert, Martin. *Israel: A History.* New York: HarperCollins, 1998.
2. Karsh, Efraim. *The Arab-Israeli Conflict: The Palestine War 1948.* Oxford: Osprey Publishing, 2002.
3. Morris, Benny. *1948: A History of the First Arab-Israeli War.* New Haven: Yale University Press, 2008.
4. Laqueur, Walter. *A History of Zionism.* New York: Schocken Books, 1972.
5. Cohen, Hillel. *Army of Shadows: Palestinian Collaboration with Zionism, 1917-1948.* Berkeley: University of California Press, 2008.
6. Khalid al-Azm. *Memoirs of Khalid al-Azm.* Damascus, 1972.
7. Begin, Menachem. *The Revolt: Story of the Irgun.* New York: Nash Publishing, 1977.
8. Teveth, Shabtai. *Ben-Gurion and the Palestinian Arabs: From Peace to War.* Oxford: Oxford University Press, 1985.
9. Wasserstein, Bernard. *The British in Palestine: The Mandatory Government and the Arab-Jewish Conflict 1917-1929.* Oxford: Basil Blackwell, 1978.
10. Bundesarchiv, Bild 146-1987-004-09A. Photograph of the Grand Mufti with Adolf Hitler, Berlin, 1941. Heinrich Hoffmann / CC-BY-SA 3.0.
11. Gabbay, Rony E. *A Political Study of the Arab-Jewish Conflict: The Arab Refugee Problem (A Case Study).* Geneva: Librairie Droz, 1959.
12. United Nations General Assembly. Resolution 181. "Plan of Partition with Economic Union," November 29, 1947.

Chapter 7: The Invention of Palestinian Identity

1. Khalidi, Rashid. *Palestinian Identity: The Construction of Modern National Consciousness*. Columbia University Press, 1997.
2. Morris, Benny. *1948: A History of the First Arab-Israeli War*. Yale University Press, 2008.
3. Smith, Charles D. *Palestine and the Arab-Israeli Conflict: A History with Documents*. Bedford/St. Martin's, 2016.
4. Rubin, Barry. *The Transformation of Palestinian Politics: From Revolution to State-Building*. Harvard University Press, 1999.
5. Aburish, Said K. *Arafat: From Defender to Dictator*. Bloomsbury Publishing, 1998.
6. Clinton, Bill. *My Life*. Knopf, 2004.
7. "The Palestinian National Charter (1964)." Palestine Liberation Organization.
8. Pipes, Daniel. *The Hidden Hand: Middle East Fears of Conspiracy*. St. Martin's Press, 1996.
9. Kuperwasser, Yossi, and Eran Lerman. "The Soviet Role in Creating the PLO and Shaping the Palestinian Narrative." Jerusalem Center for Public Affairs, 2014.
10. Karsh, Efraim. *Arafat's War: The Man and His Battle for Israeli Conquest*. Grove Press, 2005.

Chapter 8: The Perpetuation of the Palestinian Problem

1. Benny Morris. *1948: A History of the First Arab-Israeli War*. Yale University Press, 2008.
2. Eugene Rogan. *The Arabs: A History*. Basic Books, 2009.
3. Rashid Khalidi. *The Hundred Years' War on Palestine*. Metropolitan Books, 2020.
4. UNHCR Reports and Statistics (Various refugee crises).
5. UNRWA Official Website and Reports, including data on registered Palestinian refugees.
6. Gat, Moshe. *The Jewish Exodus from Iraq 1948–1951*. Routledge, 2017.
7. "World Bank Data on Population Growth in the West Bank and Gaza," accessed 2023.
8. The Institute for Monitoring Peace and Cultural Tolerance in School Education (IMPACT-se). Reports on Palestinian textbooks and UNRWA.
9. Middle East Media Research Institute (MEMRI). Investigative reports on UNRWA's role and indoctrination.
10. Bernard Wasserstein. *Israel and Palestine: Why They Fight and Can They Stop?* Yale University Press, 2003.
11. Kuperwasser, Yossi, and Lerman, Eran. "UNRWA's Role in Perpetuating the Palestinian Refugee Problem." Jerusalem Center for Public Affairs, 2020.

Chapter 9: The Rising of Hamas

1. Matthew Levitt. *Hamas: Politics, Charity, and Terrorism in the Service of Jihad.* Yale University Press, 2006.
2. Jonathan Schanzer. *Hamas vs. Fatah: The Struggle for Palestine.* Palgrave Macmillan, 2008.
3. Shaul Mishal and Avraham Sela. *The Palestinian Hamas: Vision, Violence, and Coexistence.* Columbia University Press, 2006.
4. Hamas Charter (1988). Official text.
5. "Children in Hamas Summer Camps Trained for Jihad." *Middle East Media Research Institute (MEMRI),* 2016.
6. Amos Harel and Avi Issacharoff. *34 Days: Israel, Hezbollah, and the War in Lebanon.* Palgrave Macmillan, 2008.
7. United Nations Office for the Coordination of Humanitarian Affairs (OCHA). Reports on Gaza.
8. U.S. Department of State. *Country Reports on Terrorism,* various years.
9. *Iran's Axis of Resistance.* Congressional Research Service, 2023.
10. Claudia Rosett. "UNRWA's Role in Hamas's Militarization." *Jerusalem Center for Public Affairs,* 2022.
11. Report by Amnesty International on LGBTQ+ persecution in Gaza under Hamas.

Chapter 10: The War in Gaza - Is It Really a Genocide?

1. Shapira, Anita. *Israel: A History.* Brandeis University Press, 2014.
2. Byman, Daniel. *A High Price: The Triumphs and Failures of Israeli Counterterrorism.* Oxford University Press, 2011.
3. Kuperman, Alan J. "The Limits of Humanitarian Intervention: Genocide in Rwanda." Brookings Institution Press, 2001.
4. UN Office for the Coordination of Humanitarian Affairs (OCHA). Reports on Gaza, various years.
5. Israeli Defense Forces (IDF). "Reports and Briefings on Hamas's Use of Human Shields," 2023.
6. "Human Shields: Hamas's Strategy in Urban Warfare." International Institute for Counter-Terrorism (ICT), 2022.
7. Erlich, Reuven. *The Use of Civilian Settings by Hamas in the Gaza Strip.* Intelligence and Terrorism Information Center, 2021.
8. BBC News. "October 7, 2023: Timeline and Aftermath," 2023.
9. Amnesty International. *Reports on Civilian Casualties in Gaza,* 2023.
10. Pollock, David. "Egypt's Role in Gaza's Crisis." The Washington Institute for Near East Policy, 2023.
11. Clinton, Bill. *My Life.* Knopf, 2004 (Insight on Middle East Peace Talks).

Chapter 11: Is Anti-Israel Sentiment the New Face of Antisemitism?

1. Marcus, Kenneth L. *The Definition of Anti-Semitism*. Oxford University Press, 2015. Examines the intersection of antisemitism and anti-Israel sentiment in modern discourse.
2. Laqueur, Walter. *The Changing Face of Anti-Semitism: From Ancient Times to the Present Day*. Oxford University Press, 2006. Traces the evolution of antisemitism and its contemporary manifestations.
3. Pew Research Center. "Global Attitudes Towards Israel and Palestine." Pew Research Center, 2019. Surveys global perceptions of Israel compared to other conflicts, highlighting disparities.
4. Küntzel, Matthias. *Jihad and Jew-Hatred: Islamism, Nazism, and the Roots of 9/11*. Telos Press, 2007. Analyzes the ideological links between Islamist and Nazi-era antisemitism.
5. United Nations General Assembly Documentation Center. Resolutions Database. UN Documentation Center, accessed 2024. Comprehensive record of UN resolutions and voting patterns concerning Israel.

Chapter 12: The Genetic Case

1. Haber, Marc et al. "The Genetic History of the Southern Levant." *Cell*, vol. 181, no. 5, 2020, pp. 1146-1157.e11. DOI: 10.1016/j.cell.2020.04.002. A comprehensive study analyzing ancient DNA from the Levant and its connection to modern populations.
2. Behar, Doron M., et al. "The genome-wide structure of the Jewish people." *Nature*, vol. 466, no. 7303, 2010, pp. 238-242. DOI: 10.1038/nature09103. Explores the genetic structure of Jewish populations, highlighting their shared Middle Eastern ancestry.
3. Ostrer, Harry, and Kenneth Skorecki. "The population genetics of the Jewish people." *Human Genetics*, vol. 132, no. 2, 2013, pp. 119-131. DOI: 10.1007/s00439-012-1235-6. Discusses genetic continuity among Jewish populations and their shared Levantine origins.
4. Moorjani, Priya, et al. "The history of African gene flow into Southern Europeans, Levantines, and Jews." *PLoS Genetics*, vol. 7, no. 4, 2011, e1001373. DOI: 10.1371/journal.pgen.1001373. Examines genetic admixture events affecting Jewish and Levantine populations.
5. Skorecki, Kenneth, et al. "Y-chromosome evidence for a founder effect in Ashkenazi Jews." *Nature Genetics*, vol. 20, no. 3, 1998, pp. 265-269. DOI: 10.1038/3105. Focuses on the genetic markers tracing the origins of Ashkenazi Jews.
6. Hammer, Michael F., et al. "Jewish and Middle Eastern non-Jewish populations share a common pool of Y-chromosome biallelic haplotypes." *Proceedings of the National Academy of Sciences*, vol. 97, no. 12, 2000, pp. 6769-6774. DOI:

10.1073/pnas.100115997. Provides evidence of shared ancestry between Jewish and Levantine populations.

7. Jenkins, Richard. *Social Identity.* 4th ed., Routledge, 2014. A broader sociological perspective on identity formation, including the role of genetic narratives in national identities.

8. Al-Zahery, Nadia, et al. "Tracing the history of the Middle East through the Y chromosome." *American Journal of Human Genetics*, vol. 80, no. 4, 2007, pp. 1155-1162. DOI: 10.1086/513477. Analyzes genetic markers across Middle Eastern populations, shedding light on historical migrations.

Chapter 13: Israel as a Democracy

1. Meir, Golda. *My Life.* Dell Publishing, 1975. An autobiography by Israel's fourth prime minister, offering insights into Israel's pursuit of peace and resilience in the face of conflict.

2. Morris, Benny. *1948: A History of the First Arab-Israeli War.* Yale University Press, 2008. A detailed account of Israel's founding and its efforts to establish peace despite regional opposition.

3. Peres, Shimon, and Arye Naor. *The New Middle East.* Schocken Books, 1993. Explores Israel's peace agreements with Egypt and Jordan and its vision for regional cooperation.

4. Klein Halevi, Yossi. *Letters to My Palestinian Neighbor.* Harper, 2018. A compelling dialogue exploring Israeli identity and its commitment to coexistence.

5. Start-Up Nation: The Story of Israel's Economic Miracle, by Dan Senor and Saul Singer. Twelve, 2009. Chronicles Israel's transformation into a global innovation hub.

6. Pogrund, Benjamin. *Drawing Fire: Investigating the Accusations of Apartheid in Israel.* Rowman & Littlefield, 2014. A critical examination of claims against Israel, focusing on its inclusive society.

7. Pipes, Daniel. *The Long Shadow: Culture and Politics in the Middle East.* Transaction Publishers, 1989. Provides context on the Middle East's political landscape, contrasting Israel's democratic values with its neighbors.

8. Shavit, Ari. *My Promised Land: The Triumph and Tragedy of Israel.* Spiegel & Grau, 2013. Explores Israel's complexity, balancing its challenges with its achievements in equality and innovation.

9. Ben-Meir, Alon. *Peace in the Middle East: United States Interests and Regional Concerns.* Continuum, 1994. Analyzes Israel's peace agreements and economic integration in the region.

10. Harari, Yuval Noah. *Sapiens: A Brief History of Humankind.* Harper, 2015. Although not directly focused on Israel, offers insights into innovation and societal development applicable to Israel's success story.

11. Central Bureau of Statistics, Israel. Annual Statistical Abstract. Latest editions. Provides data on Israel's economic growth, demographic diversity, and societal development.

To the victims of October 7, their families, and the hostages who endured unimaginable hardship,

To the brave IDF soldiers who fight valiantly on all fronts, defending Israel with courage and sacrifice,

And to my daughter—may this book help you embrace facts over fiction and inspire a lifelong pursuit of truth in a world often clouded by narratives.

www.ingramcontent.com/pod-product-compliance
Lightning Source LLC
LaVergne TN
LVHW011325080426
835513LV00006B/202